Hidden Truths

The Magic of Mysticism and I_________________ons

*Eight Spiritual Laws of the Universe
and How They Can Work for You*

Published by Mindstir Media, LLC
45 Lafayette Rd | Suite 181| North Hampton, NH 03862 | USA
1.800.767.0531 | www.mindstirmedia.com

Printed in the United States of America
ISBN-13: 979-8-9856345-1-8

Hidden Truths

The Magic of Mysticism and Its Modern-Day Applications

*Eight Spiritual Laws of the Universe
and How They Can Work for You*

Dr. Frances Yahia

Contents

Introduction

THIS BOOK THAT YOU ARE ABOUT TO READ will hopefully change your life. In it I share many of the things I've learned as a student of the esoteric. I hope you will enjoy it, and that you will benefit from its offerings so that your spiritual life may flourish and grow.

I have always had spiritual yearnings, as so many of us do. However, I was born into a cult and always thought I needed an intermediary between myself and what I considered God to be. The cult leader had many mediums who were studying under her, yet she kept them tied down and never let them fully develop, nor did she let them leave her side. I was forced into an arranged, abusive marriage with her nephew and had three children with him. When they were in diapers, I finally got enough courage to leave him and the cult.

Shortly thereafter I started dating another spiritual medium who helped me develop my spiritual gifts, but he himself wasn't applying spirituality properly as I understood it, so I broke it off. One evening I voiced a primal scream and yelled at God, "If you exist, show me!!!" At that exact moment, The Zohar, a book about Kabballah, fell off my shelf and opened up to a quote that changed everything for me. "There is no coercion in spirituality."

At that moment I realized I had never known true spirituality. I packed up my altar, threw everything in the dumpster, and sat in silence, waiting for answers. The following Sunday, I was watching an astrology program and the guest was a psychologist—who happened to be a Pisces like myself. This psychologist said that astrology was a tool he used in his practice to help his clients. I called for an appointment and visited the TV astrologer the next day.

What was supposed to be a sixty-minute session lasted only ten minutes. These were the most important ten minutes of my life. He told me I'd be divorced, which I was, and then he said, "You can be in charge of your own life." I had never heard those words before. Both the cult leader and the man I dated after that had led me to believe that I needed them to develop spiritually and to know Spirit.

I asked the astrologer how I could be in charge of my own life. He told me to sign up for his astrology classes. I started the next month. I completed a fifteen-month program in six months. I was hooked. Astrology taught me, above all, that I was exactly who I was supposed to be. Shortly after that, while driving on the highway, I heard the words *Akashic Records*. The Akashic Records are a compendium of all universal events, thoughts, words, emotions, and intentions ever to have occurred in the past, present, or future. I found a reader the next day and had an Akashic Records reading done.

The next week I signed up for her classes. I became an Akashic Records reader myself and I felt I was home for the first time in my life. After a period spent studying and reading astrological charts and Akashic Records for clients, I was led to shamanism. I was in meditation and a man showed up and said, "My name is Lonewolf and I'm your next teacher." Later that day, I was driving again and my spirit guides told me to check my phone, that Lonewolf was a real man (not a spirit), and that his name and number were in my phone. I called the number and this man, who called himself Lonewolf, said, "I've been waiting for you."

Unbelievable right? I thought so too.

I met him the next day. He had started a shamanism school in Miami and I joined it. I added Ayurveda, Egyptian tarot, chakra healings, and other modalities to my practice as well. I started noticing similar themes in all of the different esoteric/religious traditions. I wanted to know their source. Every spiritual tradition, religion, and philosophy has the same laws; they are universal laws and I went to the source. I am naturally clairvoyant and claircognizant and my spirit guides speak to me in symbol, mythology, and metaphor.

I realized that this was the language of the universe and the subconscious mind. I became addicted to studying myth and symbol! I started connecting the dots again in all the philosophies and traditions I studied. Again, I found the same messages in all the symbols, myths, and metaphors, and the more I studied, the more they kept coming around to eight universal laws.

My guides explained that the universe has three languages: music, mathematics, and metaphysics. I understood music as metaphysics through the Law of Octaves, and I understood mathematics through metaphysics in astrology. As I studied more and more, I saw the parallels—whether I was studying sacred geometry and nature's mathematical number, the Fibonacci number as spiritual growth, or the symbol of the enneagram for the cycles of the universe—or the patterns that every age follows, as dictated by the universal laws. I understood that everything follows these eight principles.

The more traditions I studied the more I understood that we are guided from the moment of conception to the last breath by these universal cycles. I was determined to crack the code! I had read *The Kybalion: A Study of the Hermetic Philosophy of Ancient Egypt and Greece* during my metaphysical studies. *The Kybalion* is a book originally published in 1908 by "Three Initiates." It is comprised of teachings of a hermetic genius, Hermes Trismegistus, who we will discuss a bit later in the introduction. My astrology teacher had introduced me to Gurdjieff and the Law of Octaves, however, I wanted to be able to apply these laws to real-life issues. To do this, I was gifted with being able to psychically download a seven-step model.

In 2016 I got my first bout of cancer. I understood that I had a mental, emotional, and physical illness and was determined to heal myself with use of these universal laws. The first cancer produced my first book, *The Seven Gates: Seven Steps Beyond Self-Awareness*. It was a game changer.

I got cancer two more times, and I wrote several more books using these laws, one for couples and one for families. The more I wrote and used these workbooks in practice with my clients, the more I realized that there is not one breath that isn't dictated by these laws. I have read many spiritual texts, yet what each book lacks is a step-by-step explanation of what spirituality is and how to cultivate a spiritual practice using these laws. They represent all of the laws of the universe, and when I applied them to my own life, it began to change.

The new age has brought a lot of information forward, however, it has also brought a lot of misinformation as well. My attempt with this book is to teach you how to use these universal laws to change your life.

If you pick just one law and create your life around it, you can achieve a balanced, stable, joy-filled life. I see clients regularly who say, "Frances, I want to do what you do." They think it's about sage, spirit guides, angels, and crystal bowls—and it's not. Dedicating yourself to a spiritual path is a full-time job, hard work, and requires constant self-analysis. I do admit I am a bit of a spiritual glutton (I want to explore everything!) and need to step away from it at times myself.

Having felt like a castaway at sea most of my life, with no map or compass, having discovered these laws, their application, and how to navigate my life using them, day by day, has literally saved my life. Without these laws, I undoubtedly know cancer would have killed me.

Spiritual growth is programmed into our DNA just like physical growth is. You're going to age. Do you want to age gracefully? If so, you probably watch your diet, exercise, and stress levels. You are guaranteed a certain amount of spiritual growth by virtue of being a spiritual being, however, with knowledge of these universal laws and a spiritual practice you can grow exponentially.

In my work I see many people devoted to healing themselves in all areas of their lives—physically, mentally, spiritually—and many if not all of them are looking to develop a spiritual practice to facilitate their growth. While they may understand that we're all spiritual beings having a human experience, they want to strengthen their connection to Spirit and so they come to me for help.

In working with so many clients over the years I realized that a great need for specific spiritual guidance exists. This great need that I saw provided the impetus for me to write this book about the eight spiritual laws of the universe and how they can be used to provide spiritual insights into one's spiritual life.

These laws include the Principle of Mentalism, the Principle of Correspondence, the Principle of Vibration, the Principle of Polarity, the Principle of Rhythm, the Principle of Cause and Effect, the Principle of Gender, and The Principle of the Law of Octaves. By familiarizing yourself with all of these laws you will be able to determine which one can best assist you and your spiritual growth.

Before we get to that, however, and before we embark on this spiritual journey together, please know that spirituality is not something you achieve; it's not a goal to get to. It's a *process*—and often the process is not a linear one and it's not a short one; it's life-long. Our spirituality, and our search for it, is inherent in our thoughts, in our day-to-day actions, in cycles we go through in life. If you can understand this, you can understand that we are never divorced from our spirituality because Spirit is who we truly are.

Many of the ancient teachings—the secret doctrines and hermetic teachings, which is what these eight principles or laws are— were sequestered away in the early days of recorded history in an attempt to keep their concepts pure, to prevent them from becoming corrupted. Despite this, many of the familiar axioms *have* been distorted and oversimplified. Today this manifests as the use of many pop words and terms when discussing spiritual matters. These are words like *abundance, manifestation, woke,* and *co-create,* to name just a few. I call this trend "Sticky Note Spirituality."

These words provide shortcuts to ancient concepts and teachings that are embedded in the spiritual laws of the universe. Current use of these buzzwords, however, tends to shrink down the real essence of the ancient teachings they are shortcuts for. It's our job as spiritual activists to bypass these buzzwords and access and maintain the integrity of the age-old teachings. In my work, I try to stay true to the original teachings so that their full meaning may be better appreciated and applied to our lives today. A major motivation for me in writing this book is to open up the readers' understanding of what these buzzwords and terms actually mean, to get to that kernel of age-old teaching from which they are derived. In short, my goal is to teach universal laws for modern-day application.

Over the years I've realized that not only do people need access to this ancient wisdom, they also need access to tools that will help them develop a spiritual practice. I got very excited when I realized that, by taking any one of the eight principles and focusing on it, a spiritual practice can be built around it! In so doing, I demonstrate how the energy of that law may be harnessed to help you. I also offer a substantive appendix, which will help you navigate your spiritual advancement. It's called The Spiritual Practices Workbook and it's filled with advice for you to guide you and aid you on your journey. Among its contents are a discussion of the twelve signs of the zodiac and the four levels of consciousness for each sign; worksheets to direct you how to benefit from Saturn cycles and Jupiter cycles; an account of the Fates and how they are reflected in your family threads and values; detailed instructions on the twelve steps of a spiritual practice; and a workbook to assist you in cultivating one.

In the book I also discuss what spirituality is and what it isn't. The book's overall objective is to demystify spirituality.

CHAPTER 1

The Foundations
of Spirituality

EIGHT OF THE SPIRITUAL LAWS that govern the universe form the basis of this book, but the foundation of spirituality must be initially touched upon before we enter into a discussion of the universal laws. So first let's take a look at the father of spirituality, Hermes Trismegistus, his symbol the caduceus, and the concept of the ALL.

THE FATHER OF SPIRITUALITY: HERMES TRISMEGISTUS

The legendary Hermes Trismegistus was a product of Ptolemaic Alexandria, a melting pot of various cultures including the Hellenistic and early Egyptian. They all had their own gods, and Hermes Trismegistus became a central figure combining, among other gods, the Greek god Hermes and the Egyptian god Thoth.

According to Manly P. Hall in his book, *The Secret Teachings of All Ages* "Master of all arts and sciences, perfect in all crafts, Ruler of the Three Worlds, Scribe of the Gods, and Keeper of the Books of Life, Thoth Hermes Trismegistus—the Three Times Greatest, the 'First Intelligencer'—was regarded by the ancient Egyptians as the embodiment of the universal mind. While in all probability there actually existed a great sage and educator by the name of Hermes, it is impossible to extricate the historical man from the mass of legendary accounts which attempt to identify him with the Cosmic Principle of Thought."

It is believed that Hermes knew the three branches of wisdom of the universe: alchemy (vibrational transmutation), astrology (the cosmos), and theurgy (knowledge of the gods). The number three relates back to the three principles in the universe that are necessary for change. In science these are the qualities of being positive, negative, or neutral. In Christianity we have the Father, Son, and Holy Spirit. In Hinduism it is Brahma, Shiva, and Vishnu. My spirit guides tell me that, as mentioned in the introduction, the three branches of wisdom are mathematics, music, and metaphysics.

We can understand the universe with any of these three analogies. For instance, astrology is all mathematics. The planets have degrees, circles have arcs, and the planets follow certain cycles and speeds. As well, the planets are separated by orbs, which determine their impact on one's life. In fact, astrology is a science of mathematical calculations of the movements of the celestial bodies and their effect on the living beings of the Earth. The enneagram is another spiritual tool that's mathematical; it tracks cycles of the universe.

Every morning I listen to the Hanuman Chalisa, a devotional hymn of praise to Hanuman, the Hindu monkey god that rules thought. I do this to start my spiritual practice for the day, to raise my vibration, and to stimulate my energy body. In mythology, the Graces and Muses also rule music, and it is through these Graces that we experience God on Earth, here and now. It is through these sensual pleasures like music that we can be introduced to the possibility of a new vibration. Our level of consciousness and vibration is established at the moment of conception. However, when we are exposed to the arts, we are experiencing God on Earth.

Finally, metaphysics is a branch of philosophy that deals with concepts of being, knowing, and the fundamental nature of reality, including the relationship between mind and matter. The word *metaphysics* comes from two Greek words that mean "after" or "behind" or "among the study of the natural."

Hermes Trismegistus is the father of this wisdom.

Hermes Trismegistus, depicted with a sphere, represents the hermetic principle ALL is Mind and spiritual growth is spherical and cyclical. He also holds the caduceus, the symbol representing the spiritual body, chakras, and knowledge. He is surrounded by the stars, given that he is considered the father of astrology.

Hermes Trismegistus is the originator of all spiritual traditions and all spiritual truths, including those of the *Emerald Tablet* and the *Corpus Hermiticum*. In addition to representing Hermes and Thoth (who invented writing, created language, and was an advisor to the gods), in astrology he is Mercury. Hermes or Mercury was the only god who could visit the Upper World (Olympus) and the Lower World (Hades); here he was the messenger of the gods. In the Bible, he is the apostle Paul who spread Jesus's teachings. He is also Enoch in the Quran.

He is as well in shamanism the trickster coyote who held the fire of transmutation. Indeed, he is considered a trickster god because he keeps us from truly knowing ourselves. Only when we sit still, in the present moment, and quiet the mind (he rules the mind) can we really know ourselves. He also rules the breath. When we are in fight-or-flight mode, we are not breathing correctly, however, when we breathe, we are in the present moment and are better able to pay attention to the quality of our thoughts.

A fun trick is to see if Mercury in your astrological chart emerged from the horizon before or after the sun on the day of your birth! If Mercury emerged before the sun, you may struggle a bit more to calm your mind or know yourself truly. In that case, these teachings of this book may be even more relevant for you. Also, if Mercury is in a different sign than your sun (they're normally found together on the chart), you may have a harder time getting closer to your true Self.

This image is the quintessential image depicting the realm of metaphysics. It reflects a curiosity about our world and the universe. In it the metaphysician is looking beyond the Earth to discover answers about the world and about himself.

Hermes Trismegistus is also considered to be the father of astrology and alchemy, which we draw upon for insight today.

Thoth (Hermes to the Egyptians), is the god of writing and language. He is the scribe of the gods, and the inventor of hieroglyphs and the 365-day calendar. He is credited with making the calculations for the establishment of the heavens, stars, Earth, and everything in them.

The Kybalion

As stated earlier, *The Kybalion* is a book that was published early in the twentieth century; it contains the teachings of Hermes Trismegistus. You may be familiar with it or you may just be familiar with the seven laws it discusses. *The Kybalion* is the most precise text there is on the universal laws. In *this* book we will only cover the seven laws that are in *The Kybalion*, although there are others as well. As mentioned earlier, we will also discuss the Law of Octaves, one of my personal favorites. Together these eight laws are the foundation of spiritual literature and a springboard for spiritual beliefs all over the world.

In all of these traditions, Hermes Trismegistus is, in addition to being the keeper of wisdom, a messenger delivering divine messages to the divinities of the respective religion he is associated with.

The Caduceus

The symbol of Hermes is the caduceus. I will briefly break down this symbol. The two intertwining snakes of the caduceus are the Ida and the Pingala, which are considered to be energy channels that criss-cross our spinal column. This is the energy body, not the physical body, but it resembles the physical body. The spinal column is called the sushumna.

Although it's the symbol of Western medicine, the caduceus or staff of Hermes has to do with balance/imbalance as it pertains to energetic health and spiritual health. Being imbalanced emotionally and spiritually will inevitably lead to physical illness.

Where the Ida and Pingala meet, the two snakes, are chakras and the wings are thought to be the winged sandals of Hermes or Mercury, who as we know, was the messenger of the gods. Thus, the caduceus is oftentimes a symbol associated with Hermes Trismegistus or Mercury. And it's related to the energy body; it's related to the spiritual wisdom that we know impacts our health or creates illness in the physical body related to the energy field. When one serpent on the staff—for instance the masculine principle—is out of balance with the other serpent, or the feminine principle, we have disease. (This is the premise of the Principle of Gender, which we will discuss in greater detail later in the book.)

Next, we will discuss the seven planes of existence.

THE SEVEN PLANES OF THE UNIVERSE

There is a tacit agreement in scholarly and spiritual circles that there are seven planes in the universe. They are called *lokas* in Buddhism and Hinduism.

As you see in the accompanying illustration, there are seven levels of the universe, (lower mental and manasic are one, also known as the lower mental and higher mental or the causal plane). The seven planes are the physical; astral; lower/higher mental or manasic, also known as causal; Buddhic or akashic; atmic or mental; Monadic or Buddhic; and logoic or messianic. Four of these are in the lower vibrations. We embody the physical vibration, which is where we live. The astral plane is where we dream, where we go when we sleep. There's the lower mental plane, and then there is the higher mental or the manasic plane right above it.

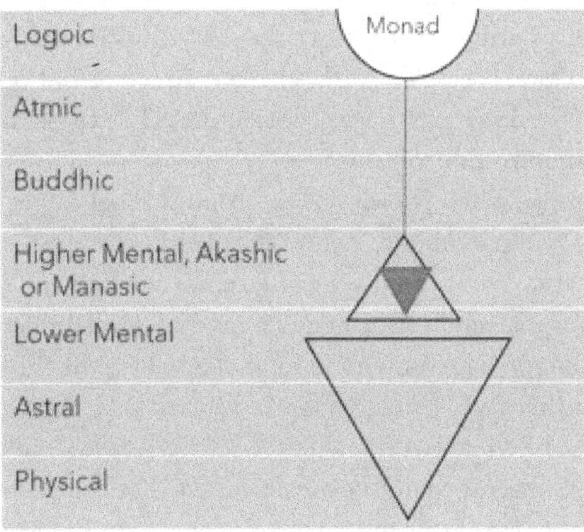

The Seven Planes of the Universe

The first four planes are the only planes that humans have access to. The Buddhic plane is often called the akashic plane, where we open the Akashic Records. We are unable to experience the higher levels of the universe while we are embodied in human form.

The four planes that humans have access to are represented by the downward triangle. This represents the feminine principle of water and earth, the densest elements. The upward triangle represents fire and air, the masculine principle, and less dense elements. The logoic plane is represented by a circle. This is the domain of ALL is Mind, and is represented with a circle because this law encompasses all the other laws. Please understand that the universe is cyclical. We view it as hierarchical because that's how we can process it, but its true nature is cyclical.

THE ALL

The universe and its seven planes comprise what is known as the one ALL. This is the overriding structure of how the universe was created. We don't necessarily have access to the ALL. This is because we're not supposed to have access to it. It's a little narcissistic and egocentric to believe that we deserve to have access to the ALL. In many traditions the ALL remains hidden.

For example, when Moses goes to Mount Sinai to get the tablets of the Ten Commandments, he can't see God's face. In Exodus 33:20 (NIV) he says, "You cannot see my face, for no man can see me and live." The Yoruba tradition contains a mythological archetype by the name of Yemaya Olokun who lives at the bottom of the ocean, and one can't see her face. Similarly, Isis in Egyptian Mythology is veiled. In all traditions, there is a version of God that one can't fully see. And that's intentional, for again, we are not, due to the density of our body, and residing as we do in this physical plane, permitted to know the ALL. We have to accept the mystery of spirituality, of the universe, within that energy field.

When we discuss the chakra system of the human body, we realize that this illustration of seven planes correlates to the seven chakras.

As such, we are a microcosm of the macrocosm. We have seven chakras—and the seventh chakra relates to the logoic plane or the monad, which is ALL in one. That represents transcendence.

You may have had glimpses of some of the higher planes. I've definitely done meditations where I've channeled supreme beings like ascended masters or archangels. These beings come down to our level in order to connect with us. But they can only sustain our lower vibrations for a short amount of time. Once when I was meditating, Archangel Michael came through. Another day it was Jesus. They come in, they give their message, and then they go back up.

It's also true that when you meditate and you feel deep emotions, you are being offered a glimpse into the ALL or the monadic. Many people cry when they meditate. They feel like they've had a vision or they've united with the Divine; with God himself. What you're doing is entering a split-second of transcendence. You're in that space. You don't actually reach this level of the monadic. But what it feels like and what it represents in our chakra system makes us feel like we are with the one, with the Divine, with Source.

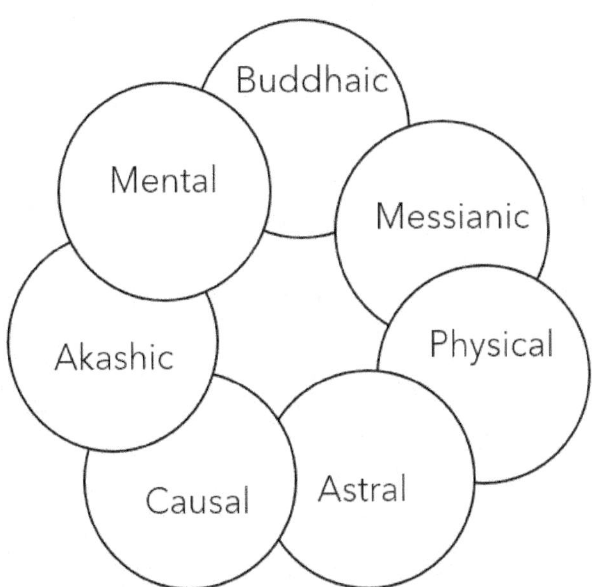

Another representation of the Seven Planes of Existence, with the attributes of each. This one is cyclical, which is how the universe is organized.

Modern-Day Theorists

Many renowned, modern-day theorists posit this idea of the one ALL. The Hungarian philosopher of science and systems theorist Ervin László is someone whose teachings I discuss when I teach the Akashic Records. He's written many books about his work, but the book of his that I most often refer to is entitled *Science and the Akashic Field: An Integral Theory of Everything*. In it he discusses the idea of one energy that oversees all the planes of existence.

Ken Wilber is a transpersonal philosopher who has many theories about this energy. There is Aldous Huxley as well; he is very well-known for *The Doors of Perception*. The famous Dr. Carl Jung, in his theory of personality, speaks of the collective unconscious and the collective consciousness that's also in relationship to the all-knowing or the ALL. Alan Watts is another philosopher who speaks to these things. If you're interested, you can read some of their literature.

Next, we will delve into the heart of this book: the universal laws of *The Kybalion* and the eighth principle, the Law of Octaves.

CHAPTER 2.

The First Law—
The Principle of Mentalism

THE FIRST LAW IN *The Kybalion* is the Principle of Mentalism and it states that the ALL is mind and the universe is mental. We just talked about this all-knowing energy. We can confirm that it houses everything in the universe. From the monadic plane to the physical plane—all seven planes—everything is mind. What you think will create your reality. This is the spiritual law that, whether we know it or not, we are held to. The concept of ALL is Mind refers to one overarching mind of the universe where nothing is dual, however, in the spiritual aspirant (occupying the earthly realm), our reality is dualistic in nature.

All is Mind

The ALL is Mind principle is emblematic of a nonchanging mind, unlike the human mind. Truth is never-changing and is guided by the universal mind. The human mind, on the other hand, is ever-changing and again, is enamored of the glamour of the world.

The Three Initiates in *The Kybalion* state, "He who grasps the truth of the Mental Nature of the universe is well advanced on The Path to Mastery. Without this Master-Key, Mastery is impossible, and the student knocks in vain at the many doors of The Temple."

In the Hercules myth of the Garden of Hesperides, Hercules is required to retrieve three golden apples. This myth addresses the matter of the spiritual initiate seeking real spiritual wisdom and trying to unify body and mind. The universe is the greatest teacher. It holds wisdom in many variations. Many doors lead to the unification of Self, to the unity of mind that the human being seeks. As in the myth, the spiritual initiate is enamored of the bells and whistles of the spiritual world. In this day and age, people would rather have more of these ceremonial bells and whistles than real spiritual understanding.

Today we are enamored of teachers and gurus claiming to have the Truth when really, we are in a spiritual holocaust. Teachers take your money and can be false prophets. If a teaching is real wisdom, a real universal truth, it will show up again and again in every tradition. This Principle of Mentalism relates to the fact that knowledge needs to be transmuted into real wisdom. If it remains academic, you are not transmuting its energy.

Hermes Trismegistus holds the hidden truths of the Universe; the ALL is Mind. The human being, however, needs to apply these lessons and teachings in order to change his or her life. This occurs when that individual is able to shift their vibration to resonate with the frequencies of the universe and live in both ordinary consciousness and spiritual—or shamanic—consciousness.

Hercules was met by Nereus, the true teacher on his path. Nereus simply nodded in the right direction, whereas Busiris—the false teacher—promised him the Truth. Hercules was misled by Busiris because Busiris told him what he wanted to hear. True teachers, like Hermes Trismegistus, Jesus, and Buddha, represent the ALL is Mind because they espouse the truth. When clients come to me and have previously been to five other healers, they're looking for the answer they wish to hear, not the truth of the situation. I call this "psychic hopping."

In the myth of Hercules, he encountered a dragon with one hundred heads. Hercules couldn't defeat the dragon despite his physical strength, because the dragon represented the mind and the dragon's mind was determined to defeat Hercules. It was only when Hercules raised his consciousness and induced the dragon to fly that he could slay him. Hercules had brute strength; however, the universe does not function at the behest of the physical, it functions at the behest of the mental. When Hercules raised his consciousness, which put him in alignment with the ALL is Mind principle, he was able to prevail against the beast.

The Four Levels of Existence

The flight of the dragon represents a rise in consciousness. Man cannot reach or understand the Principle of ALL is Mind without raising his level of consciousness level. In astrology, each sign has four animals or archetypes associated with it. Four represents the number of the material world, the Earth. Four is a number of limitation, which is reflected by the limitations of the human body. However, these four levels of consciousness represent the seven planes of the universe broken into the larger planes as in the diagram (of the planes) that we saw in the introduction: the physical plane, the astral plane, the causal plane, and the akashic plane.

Since humans are limited to the first four planes, the seven planes collapse into the physical plane, the astral plane, the causal plane, and the akashic plane to represent the levels of consciousness and how the ALL is Mind principle makes itself evident to humans.

My teacher Mauricio Puerta called the four levels of consciousness stone, water, wine, and blood. The Upanishads, which are Hindu sacred treatises written in Sanskrit circa 800–200 BCE, maintain that the four levels of consciousness are Visva (waking state), Taijasa (dream state), Prajna (dreamless sleep), and Turiya (pure consciousness).

For each situation, archetype, planet, and astrological sign you have the option of showing up in one of the four consciousness levels. For instance, the highest level of consciousness (blood, akashic, or turiya) is the representation of the ALL is Mind principle in the earthly realm.[1]

Dr. Daniel Amen's book, *Your Brain is Always Listening: Tame the*

---

1 Please see page 157 in the appendix for all twelve astrological signs and the four levels associated with each sign.

Hidden Dragons that Control Your Happiness, Habits, and Hang-Ups speaks to the neurobiology and ancestry of the ALL is Mind principle. Hermeticists, astrologers, and mystics have known the ALL is Mind principle for centuries and are aware of the ancestral loyalties, transgenerational traumas, and emotional memories that keep generations of people reliving trauma. This is the ALL is Mind principle at its lowest vibration—that of the physical and astral plane.

In the astrological chart, we see the feminine lineage trauma on the left side and the masculine lineage trauma on the right side. The astrological chart is divided into two hemispheres. The left is the western hemisphere and the right is the eastern hemisphere. All generational trauma passed on by the father is on the right side, or the eastern hemisphere. All ancestral trauma passed on by the maternal side, is found on the left, or the side of the western hemisphere. The wisdom of universal truths, or more importantly, the application of the teachings and the raising of your vibration and consciousness levels, help to make a scar of the trauma and as such it's passed onto other generations.

The highest vibration at the physical plane of ALL is Mind is the concept of epigenetics. When a person's lifestyle choices, hence consciousness level, is raised, it turns off a genetic switch for disease onset. This principle encompasses the ALL is Mind. We can stop personal trauma, cultural and societal problems, and worldwide abuses with the appropriate use of this principle.

The Practice of Ho'oponopono

One of my favorite applications of this principle is ho'oponopono, an ancient Hawaiian healing technique that a psychologist by the name of Hew Len brought back into our consciousness. As you begin to develop your spiritual practice, it would be wise to include this ancient practice in it. Ho'oponopono is a practice of taking responsibility for the life that you have created, including the pain and suffering of, not only oneself, but others too, and the chaotic world that one is living in.

Dr. Len worked at the Hawaii State Hospital, a psychiatric facility, as a therapist and, without ever seeing a patient, cured the patients there of psychiatric illness. This technique requires full presence and the repetition of the words, *I love you, I'm sorry, Please forgive me,* and *Thank you* over and over again.

Dr. Len prayed this mantra repeatedly. He was said to be working on his own spiritual development, based on the premise that he had created the mental illness in the patients in the ward that he oversaw, and thus he was responsible for it. He maintained that, by healing himself, he healed them. The results of this were that over the course of four years the inmates were cured and sent home. According to Hawaiian records, this particular ward of the hospital was then closed. This story is recounted by Joe Vitale and Ihaleakala Hew Len in their book *Zero Limits: The Secret Hawaiian System for Wealth, Health, Peace and More.*

I had a client once ask me what she could do to make the world a better place for the animals she cared for, and my guides said, "Take responsibility for the world you've created, in this lifetime and in the past ones as well."

When I see clients, I ask them to take responsibility for their problems, which were created by them. It is difficult to get buy-in to this idea. However, I simply ask that for our sixty-minute session they agree to having created the problem so that we can go to the solution. This is simply what this prayer is referring to, taking personal responsibility. Many years ago, I was in an abusive marriage and planning to leave it. I was in the shower one day and felt a hand on my shower and I heard the words "take personal responsibility."

I was in my Ph.D. program and our weekly assignment was to write my theory of counseling. I had finished my paper, but after having had that experience, I rewrote the paper and explained that having a client take personal responsibility for a problem, not in a blaming or shaming way, but in a constructive way, would be my counseling technique.

This is a premise of my counseling work and is the spiritual law I hold myself to every day: If it is in my world, I participated in creating it.

People are often confused by the concept of karma. It simply means that for every action, there is a reaction. What isn't as clear is that thought is energy, and that creates karma as well. ALL is Mind is simply a request from the universe to clean up our thoughts and stop producing filth.

Ho'oponopono allows you to take responsibility for having created the pollution, social injustice, physical illness, and anything else that is causing distress in your life: internal or external. The best way to practice ho'oponopono is when you are bothered by something (anything!), simply quiet the mind and say, "I love you, I'm sorry, Please forgive me, and Thank you" repeatedly. Think about how you may have contributed to that situation. Is there a parallel in your own life? Know that the mere awareness of your responsibility in the situation begins to change the situation.

This doesn't take long to do.

Many years ago, a dear friend called me. He was venting while I drove to work on my hour commute. I heard his story and ho'oponopono'ed him the entire drive. When I parked to go into my office, he said, "I don't know what you did, but I feel different." And when I was arguing with my (now) ex-husband he used to ask me, "Are you ho'oponopono-ing me?" because he was feeling calmer during an argument, rather than allowing it to escalate.

I find this technique of ho'oponopono to be particularly useful when I can't identify exactly what annoys me or bothers me in a person or a situation. But it doesn't matter; I just practice the ho'oponopono anyway until I feel the disturbing emotion pass. It prevents me from slipping into childlike patterns and keeps my vibration elevated, despite having had a negative reaction to that person or a situation initially.

Why does ho'oponopono work? Because of the principle ALL is Mind. We are all one and we need to raise our consciousness individually and collectively in order to heal our world and ourselves. When Dr. Len connected to the universal mind, he eliminated duality and as a result was able to heal patients in the collective. This unification is represented by the two raised serpents (representing duality) meeting one another to become one on the caduceus. When we work at a high level of consciousness and connect to the universal mind, we become like the serpents, unified in higher consciousness.

Dr. Hew Len understood this. He too had been responsible for creating the mess at the hospital. This is just one example that demonstrates that we all have the power to change the world and leave it a better place for our children. That said, rarely do we want to take responsibility for *everything* in our life. That's no fun! It's hard work, and it's the ultimate spiritual practice—no sage, bowls or crystals needed!

If Dr. Hew Lan cleaned up the mental ward of a hospital in four years, can you imagine what messes in your life you can clean up if you take this practice seriously?

Again, duality is the belief that we are separate from the universal mind. It is what keeps us in fear and limited in our thoughts. When Dr. Len connected to the universal mind, he was in unity, not duality. If we live in dual consciousness, we can't connect to the universe. It's only when we are in unified consciousness that we can hear the subtle whispers of intuition and understand how the universe is speaking to us. This is referred to as having a spiritual state of consciousness (SC).

The techniques used in SC involve examining the spiritual side of life and how or why it may be contributing to other arenas of one's existence. For instance, why did I create this situation? What need is it fulfilling? This reality tells me that I have to identify the spiritual needs attached to the story or situation. In this, I connect both to the client and to the universal mind and in so doing I am able to have insight into how the client contributed to creating their illness or problem. If the client maintains the consciousness of a victim, very little is healed. It is necessary for the client, indeed essential, for he or she to admit to how they have contributed to the creation of their problem (albeit unknowingly in most cases).

Although it's vital to be able to connect to the universal mind in this say, it's also spiritually important to honor the concerns of the body. This is absolutely necessary to keep us grounded as we go about the practical concerns of the day, such as working to pay the bills, eating, and sleeping. This is also about boundaries and being able to set them, both for oneself and for others. Thus, when I am in practice, in addition to employing the techniques of SC, I employ the techniques used in an earthly state of consciousness (EC), which place more emphasis on the practical aspects of life. This tends to focus on real-life problems so that one's life runs as smoothly as possible.

The Necessity of Grief

Einstein famously said, "We can't solve problems by using the same kind of thinking we used when we created them." If you remain in victim consciousness, even if it appears to the world that you are indeed a victim, you need to have a shift in consciousness to solve the problem that you yourself have created. When I realized that I was exactly like my ex-husband, and I had created the nightmare that was my life, I cried and cried, and then started changing my life. I am a believer that most people create situations to grieve, as a tool to process the responsibility that they've had in creating the life they're leading. Grief leads to meaning and change, because once you mourn the fact that you are responsible for your problems, you want to help others so they don't repeat the same mistakes. Grief is an earthly disease. It teaches us how we identify with earthly attachments and losing them leads us to the spiritual disease of despair, the path to deep spiritual work.

According to the Law of Octaves (which we will detail in chapter 9), when we are about to reach the second DO (of the musical scale, which is a higher octave), a grieving process needs to occur. It is often accompanied by a divorce, a death, a job loss, or an illness. We need a reason to grieve because we're not yet evolved enough to state that (for instance), "I need to grieve the life I've created, so I'll be out of commission for three years to work on my spirit."

I created cancer and a divorce in order to mourn the life I'd been living. I had permission to take three years off to lick my wounds. My hope is to be able to help clients reduce illness or unnecessary suffering. Illness in shamanism is seen as an initiation and a purification to doing deeper spiritual work, but with consciousness we can perhaps reduce the severity of the illness and pain. Instead, they should be able to simply say no, set boundaries, put themselves first, and admit that they've created the nightmare that their life has become. Someone else didn't create your circumstances, you did. I'm a believer in karma, but there are different kinds of karma.

One kind is sanchitta karma, which is the combined karma from all previous lifetimes. Another type of karma is the additional karma we continue to create by failing to take responsibility in this lifetime for our thoughts and actions. It is known as agami karma. Prarabdha is that portion of past karma that's responsible for the present body; it's that portion of the sanchita karma that influences human life today. As such, it is ripe for reaping. It cannot be avoided or changed. It is only exhausted by being experienced. You pay your past debts. Prarabdha karma is that which has begun and is actually bearing fruit. It is selected out of the mass of karma that is known as sanchita karma.

The Akashic Records

A similar version of this is my work with the Akashic Records where I connect to the akashic field. Here all information is stored—again, the highest-level humans can access. Here also is where the ALL is Mind principle is accessed from the earthly and astral realms. I can read a client's energy and speak the truth about their pain and suffering because I am connected to the ALL consciousness. The information that comes through is not filtered through my mind or the client's mind. However, I must then bring the information I receive down with words to express the energetic vibration to the client so they can receive the message. The spirit realm can only use what I have in my knowledge base.

When clients ask for intuitive techniques to learn I always direct them to study the Akashic Records with me as one of the first steps of their spiritual development. Or one can access the records oneself. There are several great books on the Akashic Records that instruct one on how to do this. My teacher Gabrielle Orr wrote an excellent book called *Akashic Records: One True Love* and teaches the same Akashic Records retrieval techniques that I teach in my classes. YouTube also has many Akashic Records meditations that can help you access your own records. Should someone learn to read their own records, words are not necessary because the ALL is Mind principle speaks in symbol, metaphor, myth, and images. In my opinion this is the best means of accessing the universal mind.

The word *akash* means "space" or "ether" and the Akashic Records are believed to store all the information that the universe contains—past, present, and future. In Indian philosophy, specifically Samkhya philosophy, the *tattvas* are elements or principles of reality. To some they are a type of deity. It is believed that tattvas form the foundation of human experience. Tattvas are used to understand the nature of the Absolute, the nature of the human soul, and the nature of the universe. Similar to the seven planes, Samkhya philosophy breaks the universe into tattvas, and the grossest level (the four lower planes), the akash, is the subtlest energy field. The akash correlates to the sound vibration or the sound *tanmatra, sabda.* Tanmatras are subtle mental elements of Indian philosophy.

Nonduality: The Ultimate Achievement

The Word that created the material world is the physical manifestation of the ALL is Mind principle. If you have ever attended a yoga or meditation class you may chant *Aum* or *Om* before class, because it represents a vibrational frequency which is the same frequency as the universe. The ALL is Mind principle, in its simplest form, *is* the universe. It is the subtlest vibration within the grossest plane (Earth) that humans have access to but is representative of the ALL is Mind principle and the messianic plane. *Aum* also represents pure consciousness or undifferentiated consciousness; the ALL is Mind principle.

The Upanishads state that the *aum* mantra is a way to bypass maya, illusion, or low-level consciousness, and connect to the ALL is Mind principle. The *aum* symbol ॐ features a crescent moon, indicating maya or illusion. The dot above the crescent moon (veil) indicates our soul and true nature, transcendence toward the turiya state, or the transmutation of thought.

When new agers use the word *woke,* they're actually speaking of the astral plane or the second plane in the universe corresponding to *svapna* or the dreaming state (a lower-level consciousness where we dream and process emotion). This astral plane is also equivalent to *maya* (the crescent moon veil represents emotions and illusion and lower-level consciousness). The point of ALL is Mind is to reach what Hindus call Brahman, the nondual state. The entire purpose of Vedanta, a Hindu philosophy based on the doctrine of the Upanishads that means the "end of the Vedas," is to achieve a nondual state. Vedanta philosophy believes that God or Brahman exists as unchanging, unlike the material world. Its goal is to achieve Oneness with Brahman. However, this nondual state is only accessible to humans by chanting the mantra *aum* ॐ or accessing the Akashic Records or other markers of high-level consciousness.

Reaching the nondual state is the ultimate achievement. In astrology the three-nine axis, the third house and ninth house in the astrological chart that are opposite each other, has to do with lower-level consciousness (represented by Mercury) and higher-level consciousness (represented by Jupiter). Unified, we can achieve a nondual state and access the true teachings of Hermes Trismegistus and the ALL is Mind principle.

In *The Kybalion,* the Principle of Mentalism states that there is always a correspondence between the laws and phenomena of the various planes of being and life. Basically, this means that if something is happening on one plane, it's happening on the six other planes as well.

Carl Jung coined the term *synchronicity* to speak about two things happening at the same time and which appear to be coincidence. He experienced this in a very profound way very personally. Here is his story from *Synchronicity: An Acausal Principle*:

"A young woman I was treating had, at a critical moment, a dream in which she was given a golden scarab. While she was telling me this dream, I sat with my back to the closed window. Suddenly I heard a noise behind me, like a gentle tapping. I turned round and saw a flying insect knocking against the window-pane from the outside. I opened the window and caught the creature in the air as it flew in. It was the nearest analogy to a golden scarab one finds in our latitudes, a scarabaeoid beetle, the common rose-chafer (Cetonia aurata), which, contrary to its usual habits had evidently felt the urge to get into a dark room at this particular moment. I must admit that nothing like it ever happened to me before or since."

This is a classic case of synchronicity, a principle I experience in my practice daily.

Hermeticists take possession of the knowledge of the unique essence of all things, and this essence of the ALL, being everywhere, is the master key to wisdom. Life itself is contradictory and paradoxical, but when you connect to the ALL, all contradictions disappear and paradoxes are reconciled, and the hidden cause of all things is understood.

Examining Sticky Note Spirituality Buzzwords Related to the Principle of Mentalism: "Visualization" and "Manifestation"

Now we will look at two common buzzwords relating to the Principle of Mentalism that are in use today and we will unpack them in order to derive their original intent and meaning. These buzzwords are *visualization* and *manifestation*.

Visualization became popularized years ago with the advent of vision boards and the book *The Secret*. Written by Rhonda Byrne about the law of attraction, her book claims that one's thoughts can change one's life. She stated that thinking about certain things will make them appear and she advocated a three-step process of asking, believing, and receiving, which she articulates in her book. As a craze, vision board parties popped up all over the globe and initially people were very enthusiastic about vision boards. However, over time, their popularity waned. When people didn't get the anticipated results, they felt as though they might be doing something wrong in the process.

To my mind, the practice of using a vision board is a worthy endeavor. Absolutely write down your goals, paint pictures of your dream house, and put your face on a model's body and stick it to your refrigerator. However, it cannot stop there.

Unpack Your Subconscious Programming

First you need to realize that you are not attaining the things you want because of the way your subconscious has been programmed since your conception. In all probability, your subconscious is filled with limiting thoughts and beliefs that originated at the moment of conception and were reinforced throughout the first seven years of your childhood. Key to understanding this is to realize that if things you envision as an adult aren't manifesting it's because you are not allowed to deviate from your family norms. When I use *family* in this context, I am primarily referring to your parents. By default, subconsciously, we are not allowed to surpass our parents. Our first step in manifesting our vision is to truly understand that we harbor this limiting construct.

How do we recognize the quality of our other thoughts and beliefs so that we can change them and thereby change our vibration? The way to achieve the results you want from your visualizations is to unpack and get to know the inner thoughts and beliefs that you've had since childhood, which are driving your behaviors today.

In my first book, *The Seven Gates* I offer a workbook that enables you to know the contents of your subconscious. There are a few ways to get to know your subconscious thoughts. As I state in my earlier book, the first step is to write down the bad qualities of your mother and father. These "bad buckets," as I call them, are the thoughts that are keeping you from achieving the vision-board reality. Better yet, make a vision board with the bad bucket items written on it. Get to really know your subconscious.

Every time you tackle one of those items on that list, things will start manifesting for you. In my earlier book I provide a seven-step process specifically on how to tackle the items on your list. The first three steps are of particular importance because they speak to the quality of your subconscious thoughts.

The first step in any spiritual tradition is correct thoughts; however, we are unaware of how to dissect our thoughts. The first three steps of my model include the necessity of, when a problematic situation appears, asking whether it pertains to the father or the mother. Next, we define why the situation makes us uncomfortable, and last, we identify why the individual created the situation. What are they trying to prove, or what issue is trying to find resolution through its expression?

Work with Your Inner Child

Another tool to defining your thoughts and the quality of your thoughts is to work with your inner child. Your inner child got "stuck" when you were seven or younger. She failed to grow up with you. Instead of a vision board, take a picture of you as a child and place it on a spiritual altar that you will construct for this purpose. If you don't have a picture, purchase a doll. If you have a baby or a puppy, you can also practice with them.

Each time you have negative-self talk, for instance, *I'm fat, I'm ugly, I'm a loser, I'm not worth it,* write out that thought on a piece of paper and tape it to your vision board. And then pick up your baby picture, doll, puppy, or child and tell them those same words. Write down how it makes you feel to tell an innocent puppy that he's a piece of trash, or your child that she's worthless. The likelihood is that you probably won't be able to do it.

However, you say this inner language to yourself all day and then expect that same inner child to get you a husband, a dream job, and a hot body! Your inner child doesn't understand the need for a sports car or a fancy dress. She is simply getting in your way, because her thought is "One more thing to take attention away from me." So, she sabotages the new and improved version of yourself that you wish for on your vision board. However, if you grow her up, talk kindly to her, and tell her you're taking her on the yacht with you, she will actually participate in helping you achieve your vision. You cannot materialize what is on your vision board if you do not observe your thoughts and identify the Principle of Mentalism in your life.

Creating Your Own Reality

We hear these words a lot today in new age parlance: *manifestation* and *visualization*. But what do they really mean, and how do they apply to the Principle of Mentalism? Because they're so closely aligned, we're going to discuss them together because a discussion of the concept of manifestation is interchangeable with a discussion of the concept of visualization.

We are creating all the time and because everything is mental, it is derived from the mind. *But this is not conscious. Again, it's all contained in the subconscious.* And every single one of us receive the programming of our subconscious mind from the moment we're conceived.

And then up until the age of seven we internalize a story that reinforces all of it. This is a very important thing to understand. Where do you think your programming came from? It came from your parents! When your soul decided to incarnate it chose the same vibration as your parents because that was your soul's vibration too.

Do you know why Jesus was born in a manger surrounded by animals? The beehive is a cluster of stars in the constellation of Cancer, called Praesepe, and it means "manger" in Latin. All souls are born into the mass consciousness and low vibration of the family, which is ruled by Cancer. The animals represent the low consciousness we inherit at the moment of conception. Try to separate from a honey pot? It's very *sticky*! But that's the soul's mission!

To leave the mass consciousness of Cancer (the family) and move into the individuation process of Leo. You cannot achieve Christ Consciousness if you don't leave the manger. Sticky Note Spirituality keeps you in the manger and the honey pot, at low level consciousness. You cannot incarnate into a family that vibrates at a different level than you. That vibration that you exhibit at conception determines the life you will lead until you decide to shift your vibration and do things differently.[2]

Whatever your parents were thinking when you were conceived, both positive and negative thoughts, became the quality of your thoughts. For instance, if your parents were upset about their careers at that moment because they felt stuck, you would inherit that same professional frustration and live it out in your career. If your mother was insecure about her body, odds are that you inherited body-image issues.

Those thoughts that haunt you were given to you by your parents when you were conceived. You will "fight" with this mind, the Principle of Mentalism, your whole life until you take responsibility for it and decide to change it. In this you can quiet the negative voices, what I call "the competitive voices," and raise your vibration so you will react more constructively in various situations.

Your story from conception is your story for life. While you cannot change the story, you can use your conscious mind to change your *reaction* to what is happening in your environment. However, if you're not aware of what's in your subconscious, your fate is going to be determined for you. As Carl Jung said, "Until you make the subconscious conscious, it will direct your life and you will call it fate."

Michael Meade, in his book *Fate and Destiny: The Two Agreements of the Soul,* discusses how you have limitations based on your family and from this fated destiny of your family origin story, your individual destiny emerges. He understands that we are limited in our ability to visualize and manifest, and because of this we must honor our subconscious and our creation myth.

You are creating your reality. You are manifesting but you're not manifesting what you put on your vision board—because that's conscious. You change as a result of making the contents of your subconscious mind known to you and then embracing them. Luckily, we have tools to identify why we're creating what we're creating and why we're manifesting what we're manifesting. This is not a conscious

---

2 I will discuss this more later in the chapter on the Principle of Rhythm. Suffice it to say here that the Principle of Rhythm follows cycles, including opportunities to change your vibration from the moment of conception.

activity. And that's what's been explained to new agers as if it is. Buddha stated, "All that we are is a result of all that we have thought."

What's Your Problem?

This is a very sensitive thing for me in practice because I typically ask the client to buy into the idea that they're manifesting what's happening in their life. Because most if not all people who seek out therapy have problems, my clients usually have a lot of problems. In working with them and trying to get them to understand that everything derives from the mental plane, I don't want to sound insensitive to their problems by telling them that they themselves are the cause of them. I understand they might be in a very difficult situation.

This is not about blame. This is not about shame. This is not about, "Oh my god, I created this because I'm being punished." It's none of that. The truth is that most people don't know the quality of their thoughts and that's why they're suffering. They're suffering from a lack of awareness. It's because they don't know that they're creating these troubling situations. We do unfortunately create from the lowest level of consciousness and we can only create from the level of consciousness our parents gave us at conception.

Changing our level of consciousness is a conscious effort, however, and you must understand ALL is Mind and the planes of the universe and the four levels of consciousness in order to choose differently. Human beings are on the physical plane. Don't kid yourself that we are creating from a monadic or even an akashic or even a higher mental plane. We are the lowest density. Therefore, what we create, what thoughts we put out, unless we become aware of them, are of low vibration.

The Bible says, "The haves will have more, and the have-nots will have less," which seems very unfair (Matthew 13:12 [NIV]). Whoever has will be given more, and they will have abundance. And others with very little will have that small portion taken away. Why is it that the superrich tend to have more and more and more, and those who are impoverished tend to have less and less and less? It's due to a mindset of scarcity or abundance, or exaggeration, or weakness, that emerges from the subconscious mind. It's learned behavior. That's what we're talking about. You create more because that's what your subconscious programming is. And if you think less or are in a state of scarcity, then you'll have less.

The Shri Yantra, symbol of the point in which all manifestation emerges

Visualizing Manifestation

The Shri Yantra is a symbol of manifestation. It is also a depiction of the universe. And in the middle, there is a tiny, tiny, tiny dot, called a bindi, which represents the subconscious mind. If you've ever been to India or you've been to an Indian religious service, you'll see that as part of the ritual, some sandalwood is put on one's third eye. The third eye is located in the sixth chakra in the middle of the forehead between our physical eyes. And the reason that's a practice in Hinduism is because of this exact depiction, which is called the Shri Yantra. This is a physical representation of the manifestation of the universe. And it always starts with a thought. On the cover of my book *The Seven Gates* I have a Shri Yantra symbol that I actually created myself.

It has the same energy and concept as the original, yet I added my own twist to it because my model of it is slightly different.

Remember—everything derives from the subconscious. The triangles of the Shri Yantra are what you're creating. The four doors of the Shri Yantra are the earthly plane representing the Tropic of Cancer (summer solstice), the Tropic of Capricorn (winter solstice), and the spring and autumnal equinox. For people who are into shamanism, they're the four directions.

We are limited by the physical plane. But everything within our body is created from one thought. If you know your thoughts, you know why you're visualizing what you're visualizing, why you're creating what you're creating, why you're manifesting what you're manifesting. Change your thoughts and you change your whole life. And this is a beautiful depiction of that in one symbol. It's a really great mandala to meditate on and I encourage you to do so.

A student once asked me, If Ascended Masters like Jesus can visit the akashic plane, can *we* visit the higher planes? The answer is no. Again, as humans we only have access to the lowest four planes of the universe, which are made up of the five elements. The higher planes are more subtle than these elements and since we humans are in a dense form, we don't have access to them.

We can only visit up to the level of the Akashic Records to glean information. However, this fourth level is representative of the entire universe and the ALL IS MIND principle. It should also be noted that in every tradition of philosophy, the creation of the world starts with the akash. For instance, John 1:1 is the first verse in the opening chapter of the Gospel of John in the New Testament of the Christian Bible. The verse reads: "In the beginning was the Word, and the Word was with God, and the Word was God."

The *Word* refers to "akash," or "ether." The remainder of Creation follows the rest of the elements in order of denseness: air, fire, water, earth. In no philosophy are there elements other than these five. Again, everything beyond the akash is beyond our grasp.

The earliest Hindu sacred writings, the Vedas, describe the seven lokas (regions) above Earth (heaven), on Earth, and the seven lokas below Earth (netherworld). The most common division of the universe is the tri-loka, or the three worlds (heaven, earth, netherworld) each which is divided into seven regions. This is linked to the principle of karma and associated with good and bad deeds in a lifetime, directing you to the plane in the universe you will land in after you die. When I channel Spirit, it's really quite interesting that I can usually tell by their "feel" if they're in the astral plane or the mental plane or which loka they reside in.

For instance, when I channel spirits, a spirit who comes in very apologetic or who is crying may be in the astral plane, the plane of emotion. That spirit that is still bound to the earthly realm, or on the other hand, may have died suddenly and not even be aware they're out of the body. This is depicted in the movie *The Sixth Sense* where the character played by Bruce Willis didn't know he was dead.

I teach to the elements, as most of us have a preferred elemental "language." This can be found in the astrological chart and the Myers Briggs personality profile. If I speak a certain language, for instance Earth, I speak in terms of limitations, boundaries, or scarcity.

The spirit world is no different. If I feel very heavy in the body when Spirit comes through, I may be channeling an Earth-bound spirit. If I'm watery and emotional, it's probably a spirit from the astral plane. I once had a client who committed suicide and he said, "Frances I can see the sun, but I can't feel it!" His energy felt cold, although I saw the sun in his reading. His mother, who had died, came to him and helped him cross over into the mental plane from the astral plane.

After she had finished working with him, I felt the sun's warmth on my body.

CHAPTER 3

The Second Law— The Principle of Correspondence

THE SECOND LAW, the Principle of Correspondence, is reflected in this ancient maxim "As above, so below, as within, so without." This principle embodies the truth that there is always a correspondence between the laws and phenomena of the various planes of being and real life as we live it every day.

For instance, if you study the monad, the highest plane, you'll understand the archangel one plane below because in truth they mirror one another. The second phrase of the maxim, "as within, so without," I personally like more than the first because it's something that I use in terms of mirroring. If I see my physical environment is disastrous, it's indicating that my inner environment is disastrous too. Indeed, Matthew 6:10 (NIV) states "Your kingdom come, your will be done, on earth as it is in heaven." This verse relates to the Law of Correspondence. With its application, the universe speaks to us moment by moment.

In my first book *The Seven Gates*, I speak about Milking the Moment. Milking the Moment is a strategy I use with clients to teach them the Law of Correspondence. I also use this when I teach the Akashic Records. When I teach this, I tell students to pay attention to sensations in their body—what they hear, feel, smell, taste, and what is going on *externally*—while they're asking the records for internal guidance.

The Significance of the Fourth House and the Third Chakra

In the astrological chart, the fourth house has to do with the childhood home, however, it represents one's inner state as well. If someone has Mars in the fourth house, I know they have a violent or conflictive household, and that they too will be conflicted in their inner state of being. They probably have an activated fight response in their autonomic nervous system and no doubt have unmet needs of safety and security. This can lead to blood pressure issues and anomalous bleeding and accidents. We recreate our inner state of being in the outside world. This is the Law of Correspondence.

The third chakra is another way to express this. The third chakra is our personal power, our self-worth—it's called the "crown of jewels." I like to say that no one is supposed to live in your third chakra but you. If I read someone's chakras and the third chakra is crowded with the "other" I know there is a personal power, self-worth issue going on in that person's life.

For instance, maybe they're not letting their child grow into an adult because they don't want to lose their identity as a mother. Or they're a "rescuer" and they've put their own life on hold to care for their alcoholic spouse. The third chakra is the element of fire, and caring for others is the element of water. Water puts fire out. Jesus said in Matthew 22:36–40 (KJV): "Thou shalt love thy neighbor, as thyself." Well, most people forget the second part of the adage. They think that taking care of others and neglecting the self brings them closer to Christ consciousness.

In all mythologies there is a goddess of love and beauty, and in Greek mythology she is Aphrodite. She represents all three types of love: erotic love (associated with the second chakra), self-love (associated with the third chakra), and agape love (associated with the fourth chakra).

We cannot skip the third chakra for if we do, we may become spiritually, psychologically, and/or physically ill. In fetal development, the vagus nerve starts in the gut and then splits off into a cranial nerve that leads to the brain. We often say the gut is the "second brain," but it is actually the first brain. The third chakra cannot carry the weight of your thoughts all by itself. One manifestation of this overload is the auto-immune disorder and gastrointestinal distress that's rampant in the United States today.

Everyone is anxious to fix their gut and populate their microbiome, but what about the thoughts that led to the breakdown? In the myth of Hercules at the Garden of Hesperides, even Atlas took a break from carrying the weight of the world. He did this so that he could help Hercules gain wisdom. Without an analysis of our thoughts and what we are creating with them, nothing will change.

You are not good to yourself or anyone if you are not owning your power. Years ago, I was about to do a chakra healing on a client and my guides told me to lay outside at noon, in the Florida sun. I questioned why and they told me that my third chakra was depleted and that my client was coming for third chakra work. Because I had such little personal power, I had none to give. From the sun, I borrowed the solar energy the client needed.

You cannot love another until you love yourself. As they say on airplanes, put your own mask on first before assisting others. The way to have enough energy for another is to first take care of yourself. If your subconscious is swinging a pendulum from 0 to 100, you are not in a place of power and are not available to help yourself or another. Many traditions say this in many different ways.

Most people have a problem with the third chakra because it is also where digestion takes place. Earlier I mentioned how many people in our culture suffer from digestive and auto-immune conditions. This is directly related to self-hatred in the subconscious. It's the inability to metabolize and digest that we have internalized the shadow of our parents. It's speaking specifically of one's inner state, which emanates from the third chakra. This is your power base, and it's illustrated by the planets in your fourth house of the zodiac.

The middle way is a *dhamma,* a teaching from the Buddha, that states the need to steer clear of both extreme asceticism and sensual indulgence. As in Buddha's teachings, to avoid the extremes of self-denial and self-indulgence, we can see when we are out of balance using the Law of Correspondence: "As within, so without." If we are living in self-denial our outer world will mirror this and when we are in self-indulgence, our environment will model this as well.

The third chakra represents the fire element—the way we show up in the world and the power we exercise. It's directly related to what I'm going to discuss next: The Middle Way, or what I call "the 48 to 52." Let's break this down and unpack it.

STAY IN THE MIDDLE ZONE

I am a believer in what I call "systems." You are an individual system, your relationship with a significant other is a system, and your relationship with your family is a system (and so on and so forth). Now let's imagine that each system in your life can be looked at through the prism of "the 48 to 52."

In this, I mean that in any given situation you encounter, you are capable of responding to or behaving in a manner that is appropriate to the situation or inappropriate to the situation. Say that someone misunderstood something you said and they let you know how annoyed they are. You then reply to this accusation in a heated, reactive way. Your response could be deemed to be out of balance with what the situation warrants. If you lash out at the person you are interacting with, your actions could be said to be an 85 on the scale of 1 to 100. We really want your actions (reactions) to be in the 48 to 52 range instead. It would fall in this middle range if you'd had a more measured response to the circumstance and calmly discussed the misunderstanding with your friend instead of lashing out at him or her.

Think of this as a gymnast's balance beam, the center of which is marked off and reads: "the 48 to 52." You as the gymnast don't want to be out on the extremes of the beam. No. You want to be right in the center at all times and in all places.

The Tao, also known as the Middle Way, is a way of life that avoids extremes. Buddhism also speaks about avoiding extremes of both self-denial and self-indulgence. In the Yin-Yang, the idea is to stand in the middle of the symbol, the curved line. And according to Tai

Chi, nature shows that the path between any extremes passes through a middle way, a compromise between two extremes. In Aristotle's Nicomachean Ethics there is a golden mean between the extremes.

In my model I call this golden mean "the 48 to 52." This is the midpoint between the 0 to 100, the place at which you will find balance and equanimity in all things. Equanimity is a state of psychological stability and composure that's undisturbed by experience or exposure to emotion, pain, or other phenomena that may cause an imbalance in thought and thus in behavior. If your parents were poor, and you're rich now to compensate for the poverty of your childhood, that's not equanimity. You didn't "win" in life, you overcompensated. These are two very different constructs.

Equanimity is about self-mastery. That's the goal of life specifically, as exemplified by the oppositions and squares in your natal birth chart. If we can achieve this with the limitations of our body, our cross, and our circle, then we can master life.

In my systems model that I discuss in all my books, I explain that the way to achieve balance in one's life, with one's partner, and in a family unit, is by way of the 48 to 52. Energy is not exact, so we cannot say 50/50, however, a happy medium is 48 to 52. This also correlates with the return of Chiron, an asteroid in the sky that represents our spiritual return home to Self. Chiron returns back to our natal placement when we are between 48 and 52 years old. It takes Chiron 48 to 52 years to orbit the sun.

Once we realize that, we understand that we are the healer we've been searching for all along.

If you have what I call "hard edges," or boundaries, you will not give your power away, or take anyone else's power. In this, you are living in the 48 to 52, which I call "sitting on your throne."

You can only have 100 percent in any given system; therefore, you must learn how to clearly design the system so that you maintain this 48 to 52 and don't give away your power. Living in the 48 to 52 zone requires that you establish firm boundaries to maintain this range. Here you are living as your true Self.

The way to truly honor yourself and others in any system is to keep 48 to 52 percent of the system for yourself. The remainder of the people in the system share the remaining 48 to 52 percent. This concept correlates to the Principle of Correspondence, where our external environment mirrors our inner climate. If we give too much in terms of time, money, or resources, we are taking from ourselves, and we are out of balance and not in the 48 to 52. Most people struggle with setting boundaries and with giving away their time and energy and resources in the name of being a good person.

This brings up an important point: I don't believe in being selfless. I believe in the big Self with a capital S, and in being selfish. Being your Self is defined as owning your own power and not taking another's power. Being selfish is when you don't own your own power (oftentimes considered to be "selfless") and you take another's power.

Later in the book I will discuss this concept of the 48 to 52 in greater detail so that you will be more readily able to apply its wisdom to your own life.

Examining Sticky Note Spirituality Buzzwords Related to the Principle of Correspondence: "Cultivate Abundance"

What does this phrase *cultivate abundance* mean in its essence, and what's wrong with it?

Also, how also does it apply to the Principle of Correspondence? I mentioned before that the bindi represents the subconscious mind. Your subconscious programming is what determines whether or not you have abundance or scarcity. It has nothing to do with the universe providing as is implied by new agers. It is hard to reprogram the subconscious and shift the loyalties that come from subconscious limitations imposed upon you by your parents from the moment of conception.

Jupiter in the astrological chart is abundance and Saturn is scarcity or limitation and we were given both types of programming at conception. In mythology, Jupiter (abundance) dethroned his father Saturn (scarcity). Jupiter represents how and where we may surpass our parents. This is often linked to the areas of finances and spiritual wisdom, for without inner wisdom you may not identify the programming that's running your life or give yourself permission to change it.

Oftentimes people with abundant mindsets, like myself, are gluttonous. Gluttony is someone who is eager for something, or who cannot get enough of something. Gluttony is a deadly sin and it poses a problem. Unless, that is, we call in the construct of the 48 to 52. Here we can strike a healthy balance, seeking the midpoint of how the dynamics of both Jupiter and Saturn play out in our lives—not overdoing it on the abundance front and ensuring that we have "enough" to get our needs met.

In this, it's important to understand that there's plenty for everyone, including yourself. Everyone wins. The story of mana in the Hebrew Bible represents this principle. Take what you need; it will be provided to you daily. Don't take more, don't take less (NIV Bible Exodus 16:1–36 and Numbers 11:1–9). The Quran 2:57, 7:160, and 20:80 also speak of mana: "Allah sent mana to the people of Israel through Moses, and its juice was a medicine for the eye." Eyes are symbolic of the paternal and maternal programing of the subconscious, which is either abundance or scarcity. The eyes also represent the fire element, or the pitta energy in Ayurveda. The fire element is linked to the third chakra of self-worth. When you live in the 48 to 52 you take what you need and leave the rest for others.

Inner Spiritual Abundance

An abundant mindset has little to do with material abundance. Instead, it's an inner peace that derives from your belief that you're worthy. It's imperative to understand that material abundance is not spiritual abundance. You can have a scarcity mindset, like several of my clients, and still be wealthy. This may be what you want, which is okay, but it's not reflective of spiritual growth. In the Bible Mark 12:17 (NIV) Jesus said to the Romans, "Give back to Caesar what is Caesar's and to God's what is God's."

We need to nourish matter, yes, but we also need to nourish the spirit. The myth of Hercules riding the Cretan bull speaks to this principle. Hercules must ride the Cretan bull to the temple. When we control the bull, the material desires, in a balanced way, we can nourish the spirit. We must do both equally by living in the 48 to 52. If you give more to the spirit or the matter, that's imbalance that needs to be balanced.

You may have a large bank account, however, if your scarcity principle is in effect your body will crumble and your outer life will manifest the scarcity. This is the Principle of Correspondence. Excess and scarcity are equal. Look past the material—the money, the paycheck—which is material, the earthly vision. When the Quran states the mana is medicine for the eyes, it is mandating that you seek spiritual wisdom, a clear seeing of what is really there, not what the person or the material world values and wants you to see. See beyond the veil. The Principle of Correspondence, when applied correctly, always shows you what is really there; it defines the truth of a situation.

If you use this in your life—asking, What is this person, place, or thing mirroring in me? you will see the real issue blocking your spiritual growth, not what you're showing the world. The psyche is conniving. I always say the psychological homeostasis harms you; it keeps you stuck. The physical homeostasis tries to help you, but not the mind. You need this principle to see clearly.

So, what's wrong with this phrase *cultivate abundance?* There's a prevailing concept that the universe abhors a vacuum: If there is a lack, the universe will provide whatever is necessary to fill that vacuum. The universe doesn't like empty spaces, neither does the mind or the body. This is true, but the universe will not fill up the void with something of a better quality than what was removed. If you don't rewrite your script around abundance from the subconscious script you were given at conception the universe will fill the space with the old programming.

You can't remove something and not replace it. Most people don't know how to replace new subconscious thoughts or rewrite the script so that abundance (and other areas of life) will change. I see a family of very wealthy women, (they are clients of mine) however, their programming is of scarcity. Wealth is not abundance. The subconscious mind, living without fear that it will be provided for, reflects an abundant mindset. In Matthew 6:28 (World English Bible) Jesus spoke in his famous Sermon on the Mount parable about the lilies of the field. "Why are you anxious about clothing? Consider the lilies of the field, how they grow. They don't toil, neither do they spin." This is a reference to understanding that if we change our minds, we will have plenty as needed. However, if we live in a scarcity mindset, we believe that the little we have is going to be taken from us.

In my first book, *The Seven Gates*, I discuss the dysfunctional version of love given to us at conception by our parents and continuing on throughout the pregnancy. This limited love may be reflected in one's astrological moon sign. We refuse to give up this limited version of love, which lacks everything on all fronts, in exchange for self-love, which is the only love capable of being unconditional and unlimited. This is what Jesus is inviting you to become.

Assume the Throne of the Void

An abundant mindset is linked to the third chakra, which then in turns shifts the sixth-chakra programming given that the third chakra and the sixth chakra are closely related. In the sixth chakra is a two-petal lotus, representing mother and father. The circle in the middle is called the void. It is called a void not because we can ever really stop our thoughts, but because we can never properly take charge of those thoughts. Assume the throne of the void. In so doing, honor your parents who are seated beside you—they gave you your programming at conception. Regardless, assume the throne and become the king or queen of your thoughts. Change a scarcity mindset, through self-love and self-forgiveness, to an abundant mindset. When you rely on yourself to provide, and I do not mean financially, rather spiritually, you can reverse a scarcity mindset.

The three women clients I referred to earlier are, as mentioned, exceptionally wealthy, however, their programming is a mindset of scarcity. We have pendulum swings in the subconscious to either accept or deny the programming we were given at conception. If you are pleased with your programming, it poses no trouble, it stays at 0. However, if the programming you were given creates an incongruence in your psyche, as with these three women, your pendulum will swing in the exact opposite direction, to 100. In so doing, it will appear in the world that you have changed your programming, but you haven't.

The Principle of Rhythm states that opposites are equal. In this particular case all three ladies have severe structural issues with their body. The structure is the foundation of the body, what holds it up. Our thoughts are what hold us up, and what create illness. These women's bodies are crumbling because they can no longer sustain the falseness and weight of the scarcity mindset.

Jupiter Cycles

We are given a chance every twelve years to shift our programming specifically around abundance. Jupiter, the planet of abundance, cycles around the sun every twelve years. Jupiter rules our spiritual growth and the abundant mindset. At twelve years old we subconsciously realize that our parents are not "gods," nor are they perfect. You may consciously know this, however, your inner child doesn't. The age of twelve is typically when a child receives the backstory behind their programming. You were gifted this mindset at conception, but now you've got a story to back it up.

At fourteen, you have your first opportunity to dethrone your parents' value system around abundance or scarcity, but you don't have permission to do so. Rather you get scolded for dating, sneaking out, hanging out with your friends. Developmentally we understand this as an adolescent storm, however, what we are really trying to do spiritually is find the 48 to 52 midpoint between abundance and scarcity and assume the mantle of our own value system. Your parents are only spiritually responsible for you until you reach the age of fourteen.

At the age of fourteen you are granted your karmic destiny for this lifetime. Up until this moment you were under your parent's spiritual umbrella. At twelve, the universe granted you the opportunity to choose your spiritual growth "story," and this cycle repeats every twelve years. You will build on this story every twelve years and grow exponentially as a result.

For instance, in 2009 I had my Jupiter return and landed my dream job as dean of the nursing school, I wrote my Ph.D. dissertation, met my then-partner, found astrology, and started my full-fledged spiritual practice. In 2021, my next Jupiter return brought me a teaching position. I also wrote four books, met my now-partner, started a metaphysical college, and grew my spiritual practice.

If you track your Jupiter cycles starting from the age of twelve, you can see the thread of your spiritual progress and shift it as necessary. Yes, it's related to material wealth many times, given that financial abundance is linked to self-worth in the psyche. However, it is really about the thread that's linked to your spiritual growth. It's unfortunate that we do not have a deeper knowledge of these cycles of Jupiter so that we may glean optimal growth from them; instead, we focus on the wealth aspect and call that growth.

My astrology teacher used to say that Jupiter would bring you whatever you wanted financially, but he (Jupiter) didn't worry about the logistics to support the gift. For instance, Jupiter will give you the million-dollar house, however, he isn't worried about how you're going to pay the mortgage! If you do not have the income to sustain the house, he will bring your scarcity or abundance mindset to light.

The notion that the universe will provide is very infantile, and it reflects a detached state of mind wherein it might appear that you have assumed no responsibility for your actions, which isn't true. I'll take you through this to show you how much responsibility and how much agency you *do* have in your life. But don't get me wrong. Determinism exists. Certain things are certainly determined for you. But your reaction or your level of consciousness, or what you create in the world, is definitely related to what you put into it. And not only as that pertains to your thinking, but what you actually do with the energy provided. We have to own our adult and stop believing that the universe will provide or that having an abundant mindset is sufficient—because it's not.

There's also an attitude that one is deserving; that one is entitled. But just because you work hard doesn't mean you're entitled to anything. If you haven't done the work, if you haven't shifted your mindset, then you're not entitled to anything. That's not the way it works. Sometimes people say, "Well, I worked eighty hours, and I still got fired," or "I barely make my bills every month and I work like a dog."

Well, just because you're working forty hours a week doesn't mean you're going to make your bills and we know this, right? I mean, this is America. This is directly related to our beliefs about what we deserve, what we're entitled to, our power, and how we own that power.

I'll give you the example of a friend of mine who has balanced her power quite well in this regard. She dabbles in real estate and she bought an apartment building with eight apartments. She and her family live in two, and she rents out six. That's efficiency; it's working for her. She's working smart, not hard. On the 0 to 100 scale, she's at neither extreme; she's somewhere in the middle. An abundance mindset, just like a scarcity mindset, is learned.

Another client of mine had a trust fund and she just wanted to be "normal." She became a hairdresser and charged very little, simply to *not* have abundance and in order to be the opposite of her parents. She had plenty, but wasn't entitled, snobby, or a baby.

Again, Jupiter in the astrological chart represents abundance, which might be very exaggerated. If you have a strong Jupiter placement in your chart, or a strong transit, you're going to be given this exaggerated, larger than life energy, which could actually be detrimental. Or this could manifest as having a scarcity mindset and therefore you manifest scarcity. Both extremes, excessive abundance and excessive scarcity, are bad programming. Again, neither one is balanced. Working our scale of 0 to 100, if we have a scarcity mindset, we can create scarcity or abundance to overcompensate. But this doesn't mean we think we are worthy.

Scarcity is not only financial. For instance, a client with arthritis or osteoporosis has what I call a scarcity disease. They may be rich but the mindset is still one of scarcity. They have a loyalty to scarcity in their subconscious. Believing you're worthy is not enough. First you must recognize that embedded in your subconscious is loyalty to your parents—either scarcity manifesting as abundance or scarcity manifesting as scarcity. Then you have to change this belief, which requires a lot of inner work, including giving yourself permission to dethrone your parents. The problem is that it's hard for us to dethrone our parents because we're afraid of losing the crappy version of love they gave us (some a bit more than others).

The universe is not a universe of scarcity, but it will *create* scarcity or abundance if you need to overcompensate. A typical thing I see in practice is someone who has a scarcity mindset will overcompensate by marrying a rich person. But if and when they divorce, they say they don't want any alimony. They say, "No, no, no, I don't want to take your money." Oh, but they do. And here we see the overcompensation.

You'll also see poverty idealized. Poverty is idealized especially for the Judeo-Christians because certain biblical passages seem to convey this. For instance, Matthew 19:24 (NIV), says, "It's easier for a camel to go through the eye of a needle than for someone who is rich to enter the Kingdom of God!" And Timothy 6:10 (NIV) says "For the love of money is the root of all of evil: which while some coveted after, they have erred from the faith, and pierced themselves through with many sorrows." We hear these axioms and we internalize them with messages like *I'm a good person, I'm going to suffer, and I'm going to have scarcity and not abundance.*

The reference to the eye of a needle is a reference to the narrow door. Most people are going through the wide door, where the masses go, doing what the crowd does, (think new agers). They do this instead of going through the narrow door, which refers to those of us who do real spiritual work, look within, take responsibility for our suffering, and clean up our messes.

SATURN CYCLES

If your mind is preoccupied solely with material and earthly gains, then you don't "fit" through the narrow door—the eye of the needle—because your abundance (Jupiter) is focused on the material (and being gluttonous; whether of food, finances, or with material possessions). However, Saturn is the narrower door, what I call "the skinny cows," which make you fine-tune your growth. A "skinny cow" period is when things slow down, life is limited and a struggle, and we need to go inward for direction and answers.

Most people do not like Saturn transits because typically they represent these skinny cows that I'm talking about. These, however, are the only cycles in which we actually burn karma, shift consciousness, and as the alchemists say, turn lead into gold. The Saturn cycles occur every seven years and they focus on what in the subconscious most needs to be dethroned. If you work the cycles appropriately, every seven years you will work through a skinny cow, a crisis, and then grow exponentially at the Jupiter cycle, five years later. The Saturn cycles build upon the Jupiter cycles and vice versa.

These two planetary cycles dictate the spiritual growth process—primarily when they work together. However, most people are unfamiliar with the link and thus they live them out separately. If we can track these cycles, we can actually plan our spiritual growth, show up with a higher consciousness during Saturn transits, and reap the rewards during a Jupiter cycle. We are at this point, both spiritually and materially in balance. (I will discuss this in greater detail in the next chapter.)

Again, five years after the skinny cow event you will have a Jupiter transit. The number five is an important number that's linked to the enneagram, and the Law of Octaves. In the European music theory called solfege, the musical notes of the scale are *Do-Re-Mi-Fa-Sol-La-Ti-Do*. The fifth note corresponds with *Sol*, which is "sun" in Spanish, which is the fire element, the solar energy, and self-worth. Jesus was not the Son of Man, rather the *Sun* of Man. This directly correlates with his true birth sign of Leo, his solar energy, and his teachings about the need to balance the third chakra by loving thy neighbor as thyself.

The number five correlates with the fifth chakra as well, which represents the etheric element linked to the Akashic Records, the highest plane in the universe that mankind is allowed to access. The enneagram number five corresponds to the year of the cycle that corresponds with growth. In the number three (*Mi*) we have thought, in the number four (*Fa*) we have crisis or limits, and once we change our thoughts, because of a crisis (Saturn, skinny cow) we then have growth (Jupiter).

The world was created with the Word, the ether, the fifth chakra, and Jupiter dethroning his father and assuming control of the heavens. When you grow you enter into the heavens, your kingdom, which is your self-worth. You will have, as with the manna, all that you need, no more no less, because you're not compensating for anything.

An Abundance or Scarcity Mindset

In physical illness we can easily see the abundance or scarcity mindset and the Principle of Correspondence at work. Your physical illness (outside) tells me about your inner world (thoughts and beliefs).

For instance, there are two types of illnesses. Scarcity illnesses are diminishing in nature, debilitating, one is wasting away, or destruction of some sort of tissue or body part, like arthritis and osteoporosis, takes place. Abundance illnesses are when there is excess growth like cancer, warts, or obesity. Both states are imbalanced, however, one is overly compensating for what may be a lack and a need to take up space or a need to be seen—because we were invalidated or neglected as children. Scarcity illnesses manifest as having a desire to shrink or not be seen, perhaps because we were scolded for being too loud, too dirty, or "too much."

But being in a state of heightened abundance or scarcity is being out of balance, which reflects the Principle of Correspondence. That's not to say that people who are uber-wealthy are overcompensating. It would depend on the situation, but there's a tendency to overcompensate when you're at the extremes.

There are limited resources on the physical plane. The currency of the physical plane is money, time, and resources. It's interesting to see people navigate their money with decisiveness, but not their time or resources. For some reason our culture condones setting boundaries around money, but not necessarily around our time and our resources, which we tend to give away indiscriminately as if their supply were unlimited.

In graduate school the hardest thing for me to learn was how to end a counseling session. As I grew my practice, I learned that charging appropriately and ending the session on time was linked to my self-worth. On my podcast *Mistress of the Subconscious,* I have an episode titled "Mind Your Pleck," in reference to knowing your place and knowing your price. When you know your self-worth, you will charge appropriately and value your time and resources.

This is simply a boundary issue. Time and resources are not unlimited. Use yours wisely. Thinking abundantly, incorrectly, has you believing there's an unlimited amount of money, time, and resources available to you, which is incorrect and naïve. There is enough for everybody absolutely and the universe itself is unlimited. However, the physical plane, where the earth element is king, is limited. There-fore, spiritual growth, maintaining the 48 to 52, is all about learning to say no, setting boundaries, and holding yourself accountable.

The abundant/scarcity mindset is directly related to your rela-tionship with money and with the establishment of independence and self-sufficiency. If you were afraid to grow up, if you're afraid to be an adult, if you want to remain a child, if you didn't symbolically leave home, you will probably suffer more from of a scarcity mindset because you're not self-sufficient. You don't pay your bills.

This doesn't mean if you have somebody paying your bills, you're not self-sufficient. If you've created a world where you're kept, that's self-sufficiency. You made that happen for yourself. There's no judg-ment there. But the fact that you don't want to grow up or you have Peter Pan Syndrome, those sorts of things are a scarcity mindset. The myth of Icarus is a good example of this. The father glues wings on his son Icarus and says to him, "Don't fly too close to the sun and don't fly too low."

With this principle, the sun is symbolic of one's power and one's potential. You can't go all the way to the sun; it'll burn your wings off. This imagery from the myth of Icarus is symbolic of our relationship with God. You can't reach those higher planes. That said, go as high as you can—don't go lower, don't aim lower. Poverty, as I said before, is frequently idealized. The scarcity mindset is linked to the seven deadly sins: pride, greed, lust, envy, gluttony, wrath, and sloth.

There's a great little fairy tale called *The Little Match Girl*. The essence of the story is that the little match girl has to sell matches on the street in order to bring money home to her family. She's freezing so she starts burning all the matches to stay warm. She's basically burning through all of her resources.

If you are not efficient with your time, with your money, with your energy, you're being wasteful and things may end badly. You're living in scarcity. Again, this is an overcompensation. The point is to be efficient with your resources and have that work for you rather than against you.

Examining Sticky Note Spirituality Buzzwords Related to the Principle of Correspondence: "I Am God; I Am the Divine"

Let's unpack this phrase *I Am God; I Am the Divine* so we can see what's wrong with it and find the kernel of original wisdom it contains. We will also articulate how it applies to the Principle of Correspondence. As I mentioned, this speaks to the maxim "as within, so without." In other words, and as we know, whatever is happening externally is a mirror to what your inner state is. I refer to the inner state as the third chakra. It houses your power and fire element, but is linked to the sixth chakra, your limiting thoughts. As I've said, we are a divine spark contained in an earthly body.

When I read chakras, I can see when someone is excessive in their belief about their god potential. In the movie *Willy Wonka*, Violet Beauregard devoured a three-course meal gumball after Willy Wonka had forbidden it, which turned her into a big blue ball given that the gumball wasn't quite ready for consumption yet. This is how people who have exaggerated beliefs about themselves feel energetically. They enter a room and their energy body knocks everything over, like a bull in a China shop.

We can feel these larger-than-life personalities and people who take up way too much space. It may correspond to them invading your space, or never letting you end a conversation even though you've made it clear you have to go. This is a mirror to your own beliefs about yourself, hence the Principle of Correspondence. This can show up in your life as people who play small and never speak up. Again, this is the Principle of Correspondence in action, mirroring abundance or scarcity.

Self-Esteem and Self-Worth

A dear client said to me once, "My biggest fear is that no one will see how great I am." However, she plays small and doesn't own her full potential. Alfred Adler spoke about the inferiority complex and the superiority complex being different extremes of the same thing.

In my podcast, I call this the "Prince or Pauper Syndrome." Those who play small feel just as god-like as those who act as if they're all that. One may reflect a narcissistic personality while the other reflects an antisocial personality, however, they're both struggling with their god complex. We are God, however, just a spark of God, limited by our humanity.

In *The Seven Gates* I invited readers to experience their divinity through their humanity. Your divinity is special. There is only one you and your humanity is your humanness, your wound and your pain.

Channel a high-vibration painful story and help humanity. That is how you channel your divine spark. In this you're fulfilled, as are others. A technique I use with clients is to have them do a full yogic breath. Put your hand on your belly, close your eyes, and take a full breath. The inhale should have you puffed out like Santa Claus; the exhale should leave you with a very flat stomach. In between the inhale and the exhale, hold the breath. Once you're done with the inhale and the exhale, identify the one you enjoyed more. If you prefer the inhale, you take up more space than you're entitled to.

You, like Violet, perhaps have gluttonous tendencies and exaggerated beliefs about your self-worth. Perhaps you feel the rules do not apply to you. If you prefer the exhale, you may play small and shrink and feel you don't deserve to take up space. Either one is mirroring the state of your mind—abundancy or scarcity—and will be modeled by those in your life.

The Oracle told Narcissus's mother to eliminate mirrors so he wouldn't fall in love with himself and die. He caught a glimpse of himself in a pond and couldn't stop admiring himself. Because of this, he eventually froze to death in the forest. Thinking we are God will result in our creating situations where we are a tyrant king and then complaining we are misunderstood and complaining about people's wrongdoing toward us. This is the Law of Correspondence in action. Again, our outside world is a reflection of our subconscious, our inner world programming, and we are creating the suffering in our lives.

We Cannot Be God

We are also not God because God is perfect, God is ALL is Mind. We, on the other hand, can only live in the lower vibrations and not surpass the akashic plane. Therefore, we cannot be God. Last, everyone is in pain because we are limited by form. God is not limited by form.

Vedanta says, "I am that." This is *Sat Chit Ananda*, which translates as "truth, consciousness, and bliss." Yes, we are absolutely capable of knowing our truth, raising our consciousness, and following our bliss, if we do undertake to do real spiritual practice.[3] However, this has been mistaken by yogis at times as being equal to reaching supreme consciousness.

Some literature purports that only a few spiritual masters have ever achieved and sustained this level of consciousness. I am not a believer that this sustained level of consciousness is possible for long periods of time. I believe some may possibly reach it, catch a glimpse, and then return to the body. The inability to understand the logoic plane as cyclical, the inability of us to go beyond the Akashic Records

---

3 Please see page 182 in the appendix for more on the twelve truths of a spiritual practices.

because of our density, informs me that these levels are not accessible on a sustained basis.

What I see in practice is that people think this state of transcendence means that one needs to disassociate from the body. This is what Ayurveda practitioners would call "Vata-vitiated." Vata is a body type made primarily of air and ether, allowing these individuals to disassociate from matter easily. But this is *not* spirituality, this is escapism and denial. Sat Chit Ananda is a state of being, of higher consciousness where you understand the universal principles yet you remain grounded in your body in utter and complete balance. In my view, we are all held to the physical laws of the universe in the earthly realm.

In yogic philosophy, a chant called *so ham* is linked to the breath. The breath in and the breath out makes the sound *so ham*, meaning, "I am that." This refers back to the unity and duality principle. "Who am I?" is a question that arises from a state of duality. But when you breathe and chant *so ham*, you are in unification with all that is. The breath is the God principle on Earth. It has been said that God lives between the inhale and the exhale. The breath is what takes us out of the fight-or-flight mode of the sympathetic nervous system so that we may make rational choices.

My spirit guides say that we fail to breathe when we don't want to pay attention to our thoughts. Therefore, we stay in fight-or-flight mode, hold our breath, react as children, and repeat subconscious programming from a place of fear. My dear friend Andrew Bloch has created TRu-BreaTH™, a simple breathing program to bring you back into the present moment, which is where all of us should be all the time. Pranayama is the fourth limb of yoga in Patanjali's *Yoga Sutras*. Remember, the number four is the earth element, the crisis. Taking a breath is a representation of letting God in on the earthly plane.

Think of the density of the physical plane versus the ethereal nature or the lightness of the monadic plane. We are in the densest plane for a reason. Do we have a spark of that divinity though? Yes. We have access to that when we reach transcendence momentarily, if even for a moment. In these instances, we release all dogma. We are past the sixth chakra—the veil—and we can reach that space in fleeting moments here and there.

You are limited to the physical plane. Ignoring your body, not feeding your body, not caring about your body—pretending as I did that, I didn't have a body—does not make you free of your body. What it makes you is sick. What it makes you is unhealthy, what it makes you is infantile, what it makes you is imbalanced. What it makes you is deranged. Just because you don't like your body doesn't mean you're free of it. And this is a very common thing in people who want to be in spirit all the time. I was this way for a long time and I got sick. You only have limited potential within your astrological wheel (this lifetime) because you're not God. This is very, very important to understand.

I was channeling Jesus the other day, and he said that this symbol of the sun looks like a bullseye because it represents original sin. Original sin simply means that we missed the mark. We missed the mark in previous lifetimes, which is why we're back here to do it again, to try and do it better this time. We are human and humans are not perfect.

This symbol is also representative of the sun symbol in the astrological chart (the one on the left). Your sun sign looks like this whatever your astrological sign is. The circle represents the cycles we are held to. These include the cycle of life-death-rebirth known as samsara, the Wheel of Fortune in tarot, the astrology wheel, the cyclical nature of the seasons, and the cyclical nature of the universe.

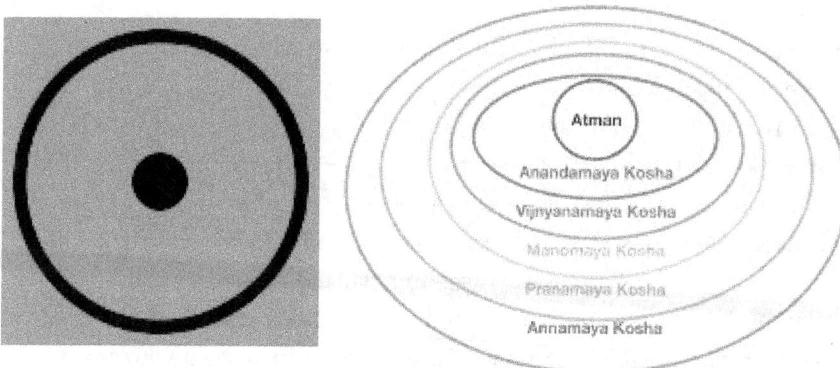

The sun symbol in the astrological chart on the left; on the right is a depiction of the Upanishads concept of the koshas.

The circle in the middle is the divine spark, self or the atman. It is covered by koshas, the five elements. The physical body, the *annamayakosha*, is the only visible one. The others are metaphorical coverings, linked to the water, air, fire, and ether elements found on Earth.

The circle to the right is a representation of the Vedic concept of the koshas. The center dot is the Atman, that divine spark. Both images represent the same thing. Yes, we have a spark of the Divine inside, but we are covered with density, what the alchemists referred to as lead. The spiritual journey is to uncover the gold, the spark of the Divine, that we all have within.

Grounding Ourselves on Planet Earth

We are born on Earth. Therefore, metaphorically and astrologically, we are born into the opposite of our sun sign. This sign is often one we dislike, because it appears to be opposite of what we are and wish to be. However, it is information for our soul about how to appropriately become the sun, or to get closer to God consciousness. For instance, I am a Pisces; my opposite sign is Virgo. Virgos are discerning, analytical, nitpicky, and tend toward obsessive-compulsive disorder because of their perfectionism. Virgos are the complete opposite of Pisces, who are carefree, not concerned with details, and are connected spiritually but are not discerning.

Pisces individuals are not perfectionists. On the contrary we lean toward low self-worth. On the surface it seems as if an Earth sign wouldn't relate to me, but Virgo energy is exactly what I need to become a full-fledged, high vibrational Pisces. *Discernment* is a key word that relates to Virgo. Discernment is what every Pisces needs in order to get out of la la land.

Many years ago, when I first started channeling, I downloaded a message to create an app. Without thinking about it, I had the app developed, spent thousands of dollars on it, and did nothing with the tool. Now, years later, after understanding spiritual messages and how Spirit works, I understand that I need discernment when communicating with my guides.

We are not here to serve the spirit. No, the spirit world is here to serve matter, in a balanced relationship. I may be guided to do something but I must consult with the earthly realm about it. Is it time to quit my job? Do I have the money to pursue this venture? If the earthly realm, money, time, and resources don't support the message, the time is not right. Therefore, I needed Virgo discernment and its connection to the body. Virgo rules the intestines and the third chakra and to really become the best Pisces I am capable of becoming, I must strike a balance between spirit and matter.

For example, Jesus was born in the body / on earth but when he died and was resurrected, he became the Christ consciousness. The SUN of God. That's your same journey. Yes, technically I am a Pisces because of my birthday, but I am not really the SUN. I was born in Pisces, but I'm the lowest level of Pisces in terms of a consciousness level, working to gain higher consciousness by rewriting my subconscious and dethroning my parents. I have to use the lessons of Virgo to teach me how to be the highest-level Pisces I can be.

I'm born of the Earth—the body, the physical plane, the koshas, the lowest consciousness—and as my journey of life continues (like alchemy) I turn lead into gold.

Again, lead is symbolic of Earth and low consciousness, and God is symbolic of the sun in the chart. Being born to the Earth, you are limited by your wheel (astrology, cycle of samsara) and you are limited by your cross (cardinal, fixed, or mutable). The cross is a symbol of Earth. The cross is a symbol of limitation. The cross is a symbol of death. In the Asian traditions, the cross in the circle represents the number four, which we'll get into a bit later. In your chart, your limitations are shown to you or to the reader of your chart. You're confined to the wheel. You're confined to this cycle and this cross in this lifetime.

The Metaphysics of It All

It's also true that you have eight lifetimes with the same people. These relationships include that of mother, father, brother, sister, lover, cousins, neighbors, mentors, authority figures, and friends. These are represented by the seven planets and the nodes in the chart. Each lifetime you incarnate into a different relationship with each of these key people. For example, your husband in this lifetime might be your father from another lifetime, based on the moon phase you're born into.

There are eight moon phases, from the new moon to the balsamic moon. Each moon phase represents an ascension of the seven planes of the universe and then a descent back to Earth again. This also corresponds to the Law of Octaves, and the notes of the musical scale that vibrate at our frequency during each lifetime (of our eight lifetimes with the same people) before moving to the next vibration.

According to the Vedas, there are seven lokas below Earth and seven lokas above Earth. After you die you go to a specific loka that corresponds to how you've lived your life. This also correlates to your moon phase, your vibration, your musical note(s), and your "planet."

Within this one lifetime the dynamics of the astrological wheel hold from conception to death. You are limited and confined to what's on that wheel for this entire lifetime. This stuff is not going away. You can ignore it but it's not going away. But remember, that's all you've got: the potential that that wheel holds for you, as well as the potential of the cross. Because again, every single one of us was born on a cross—either cardinal, fixed, or mutable—and confined to the wheel.

It's all consciousness. That's all you're here to do—grow in consciousness. And I can tell you what my guides have said and I said a moment ago: we all work at a very low, dense animal level of consciousness. And we grow, hopefully, into a higher level of consciousness. And in that, we're constantly missing the mark. If we are able, in the limitations of our wheel and our cross, to reach our full potential, and the highest expression of consciousness with the challenges we have, we beat life: We win. How? I say 80 percent but you want to go for 100? The midpoint of our extremes is the 48 to 52. The 80 percent here refers to showing up for ourselves (in the 48 to 52) 80 percent of the time. But remember, we miss the mark over and over and over again. There's a reason the spiritual path is a circle.

CHAPTER 4

The Third Law— The Principle of Vibration

THIS THIRD LAW is as follows: "Nothing rests. Everything moves. Everything vibrates. Everything has a varying degree of vibration." I have a dear friend who has moved house quite a bit since I've known her. In so doing she'll talk to her furniture, she'll talk to her books, and she'll talk to everything she owns to see whether or not they want to go with her on her move.

This expresses the idea of vibration—that everything's alive, so to speak. Einstein stated "Everything in life is vibration" because he understood this principle. This is one of his famous quotes. He wrote about vibration and frequency as science, not philosophy. He knew this law: E=mc2. The law of nature states that *everything* has a vibration. Atoms, the basic building blocks of life, are in a constant state of motion, whether they be forming a solid, liquid, or gas. Sound is also a vibration and so are thoughts. Everything that manifests in your life is there because it matches the vibration of your thoughts. If you live from a higher vibration, you can change the world around you.

The Philosopher's Stone or The Squared Circle

In physical alchemy, a metaphor for spiritual alchemy, lead (Saturn) was turned to gold, an idea that we mentioned briefly in the last chapter. The Philosopher's Stone was an imaginary substance that was created by turning this mercury or lead into gold. However, the image of the Philosopher's Stone (above) is actually a representation of the universe, based on vibration. The outer circle is the highest level of consciousness or vibration. It represents the ALL is Mind and the messianic plane.

The triangle represents thoughts and how the level of our consciousness and the vibrational level of our thoughts matches the outer reality (the square). The triangle also represents the first three principles of change: positive, negative, or neutral (which again, correlates to Father, Son, Holy Spirit—or in Hinduism, Vishnu, Shiva, and Brahman).

This is the first step in the Law of Octaves, but it has to do with thought, vibration of the thought, consciousness level of the thought, and as of yet unmaterialized thought. The inner square represents manifested thought. Again, you will create the square, your outer world, based on the vibrational level of your thoughts. Like with the Sri Yantra, the four doors surrounding the triangles represent the outer reality of your mind.

The lead in the alchemic philosophy represents the earth element, the limitation of the earth element or the world. Saturn in our birth chart speaks to where we are limited in thought; where we need a higher vibration.

The lead in the Philosopher's Stone is exactly where we need to apply the Law of Vibration. We always show up at the lowest level of consciousness, the lowest vibration, wherever Saturn is in our chart. Every seven years we get an opportunity to re-do the lesson. Every seven years we get the opportunity to turn lead into gold wherein we show up in our lives in a higher vibration so that aspect of our life can improve.

Just like in the movie *Groundhog Day* when the character played by Bill Murray shifted his vibration and his life changed, we get a chance every seven years to increase our vibration and shift our consciousness. There are three big rounds of Saturn cycles in our lifetime, assuming we live a full lifetime.

As stated in the last chapter, our initial Saturn cycle occurs when we are seven. This is where the story *begins* in our conscious minds, however, it *started* at conception. Every seven years afterward we have a skinny cow, another Saturn cycle.

How the Cycles of Saturn and Jupiter Build Upon Each Other

There are two types of Saturn cycles, those that occur at age 7, 21, 35, 49, 63, 77, and 91, which I call V-years or Valor years and neutralizers. As we know, these Saturn cycles begin at seven and are repeated every fourteen years. They are an attempt to own our value system, rather than live out our parent's values. The second type are what I call neutralizers, N-years, or Nemesis years. This is when certain people, often viewed as a nemesis, enter our path to try and teach us to slow the 0 to 100 swings. These are situations or people that slow us down. Perhaps we get fired or divorced, or we're in a car accident. These neutralizers are "planted" every fourteen years, starting at age 14, to help us achieve the 48 to 52. They occur at age 14, 28, 42, 56, 70, 84, and 98. The first set of Saturn cycles refer to the Law of Rhythm in that they represent the internal "winters" we experience. These cycles are intended to help us identify the values from childhood we no longer subscribe to and where we try to do things differently. It is our attempt to "leave home" and dethrone our parents. The second set of Saturn cycles are external. There is a person, place, thing, or situation that "takes" you from home, your parents, your previously held beliefs.

These neutralizers are external forces designed to help you honor your true purpose in life, not your parents. The most marked Saturn cycle is when we are between twenty-eight and thirty years old. Here we get the "cross we bear" for the next thirty years, oftentimes what we call "adulting." We may get married, have a child, take out a mortgage, and/or start a professional career. This corresponds with prefrontal cortex development of the brain, which is responsible for executive functioning.

This particular cycle pushes us to "leave home" and attempt to do things differently from our parents. Usually, however, we manifest the opposite behavior. It's only in the next Saturn cycle that we realize that we've actually *become* our parents. This second Saturn transit is at age fifty-eight to sixty and corresponds with retirement and enjoying our grandchildren. These are very broad examples. Obviously, your story that has developed up to the age of seven will dictate what happens in *your* life.

This cycle corresponds with grief, loss of purpose, and a search for meaning. We are confronted with mortality and we may realize we've lived an unexamined life and want to make the most of our time left. Should we be lucky to live to ninety, we will have our third Saturn return and by this time we have probably learned to set boundaries, enjoy the fruit of our labor, and look back at our life with either regret (if we think didn't do it correctly) or take a breath and indulge in the legacy we will leave behind.

This means we get ninety years in each lifetime to shift our vibration. Each opportunity of Saturn is a chance to shift the vibration that we received at the moment of conception. These cycles are perfectly timed throughout our life, piggybacked by Jupiter to help balance our spiritual growth. In the Bible, Joseph prophesizes for the pharaoh that the fat cows will be eaten by the skinny cows. The fat cows are Jupiter cycles, occurring every twelve years. As we've established elsewhere,

Saturn cycles swallow that growth and propel us into our next spiral of spiritual growth.

Navigating the Planets and Their Cycles

In mythology, Saturn was the god of the harvest. He ruled for thirty years and the crops were strong during this time. The Saturnalia, which falls on every December 25, celebrated the harvest of the year. The Saturnalia represented the concept of "reap what you sow." If you show up with a high level of consciousness within these Saturn cycles you will reap benefits of your hard work.[4] Galatians 6:8 (NIV) states, "Whoever sows to please their flesh, from the flesh will reap destruction; whoever sows to please the Spirit, from the Spirit will reap eternal life. Let us not become weary in doing good, for at the proper time we will reap a harvest if we do not give up."

Christianity displaced Saturn, replacing Jesus with Saturn, in order to represent the same thing. In our astrological chart, Mars represents our power currency and our communication style. You either have an overt power currency, which implies aggression or violence, or a covert power currency, which implies manipulation and passive-aggressiveness (at the lowest vibration). However, you can channel these into a high vibration by transmuting aggression into assertiveness and manipulation into transparency.

Even Jesus referenced this in Matthew 5:25 (KJV) when he said, "Agree with thine adversary quickly."

He was referring to a shift in one's vibration. The highest plane humans can achieve is the akasha, which is related to the fifth chakra and the sound *tanmatra* represented by speech. Our delivery of a message impacts what we create in the world.

Earlier I talked about having hard edges. The second part of that expression is "having soft corners": have hard edges and soft corners. Hard edges represent authority, clarity, and structure and soft edges represent compassion and empathy. You need both to be effective in delivery, behavior change, and spiritual transmutation. Another way

---

4 Please see page 178 in the appendix for more on Saturn cycles.

we can deliver effective speech is by taking the Principle of Vibration into account. Achieving more in our outer world is to communicate with a person at their level of vibration, what I call their "preferred element."

In your astrological chart the main seven planets are all in an astrological sign. Each sign represents an element: fire, earth, air, or water. If you tally up the planets you will get a formula for the elements. Your highest element is your vibration of preference. For instance, I have the most planets in air and water signs, so I vibrate at water and air. I am a teacher, a therapist, and a counselor so I vibrate at the air element and—I am a psychic. Because of that, and because I write about the subconscious, I vibrate at the level of the water element also.

Your Vibrational Level

Communicating with people at their vibrational level, their preferred element, leads to a better result. Every planet, illness, archetype, type of food, or chakra, for example, has a vibrational quality rooted in its elemental structure. It's easy to calculate your astrological elements for free online. If you can't calculate the entire birth chart at least focus on the element of your sun sign.

For instance, Pisces is a "water sign" (along with Scorpio and Cancer). As a Pisces I enjoy the water vibration of feelings and the subconscious. I'm more apt to listen if you speak my language. I have very little earth in my chart and I have a tendency to reject the earth element. Thus, if you speak with an earth vibration, it may be difficult for me to grasp and understand what you want, or I may resist doing things your way. The biblical story of the Tower of Babel in Genesis 11:1–9 (NIV) describes the emergence of language in the world. At its core, it's explaining vibrational language and how ego gets in the way of communicating effectively.

The vibration of Earth is dense. It is found in the first chakra. The symbol of the first chakra is the square and the square represents the earthly plane. The key words to create change are *roots, consistency, boundaries, discipline,* and *structure.* It is by implementing boundaries, discipline, consistency, and structure that behavior change occurs.

The vibration of water is second and is represented by the second chakra. The key words to create change here are *emotions, memories, needs, traditions, subconscious,* and *nurturance.*

The fire vibration is third and is represented by our solar plexus or *manipura* chakra. Key words to create change in this case are *fire, change, will, action, leadership, initiative,* and *creation.*

Air people represent the fourth vibration and key words for it include *intellect, rational thought, reading, speech, thinking, brilliance, science,* and *education.* The fourth chakra is the heart chakra. Key words are *love, compassion, empathy,* and *forgiveness.*

The fifth element is the akasha and is linked to the fifth chakra. Key words represent the *ether, ideas, wisdom, spirit, soul,* and *psychic ability.*

The Principle of Vibration is found in a psychic principle known as psychometry. When employing psychometry, we hold an object, just an inanimate object, and after quieting our mind, we are apt to receive some story or history about who made it and where it came from. This is because everything vibrates and holds energy. The longer something has been in existence, the more vibrational currency it holds. The more exposed the object has been to living things, the stronger it vibrates. An envelope at Office Depot may have a very small psychometric vibration, however, my favorite kitchen table where I've shared multiple family meals and holiday dinners may vibrate at a high resonance.

I invite you to hold inanimate objects in your home and get a read on their story. I once held a ring that belonged to a client's grandmother and I saw the ocean liner she traveled on from Turkey to the United States when she immigrated.

Everything vibrates. Everything holds memory. Everything has a story.

What's wrong with this notion and how does it apply to the Principle of Vibration?

One of the reasons I don't like the message of *positive vibes only* is that there's a judgment attached to it, as if feeling bad or depressed or the fact that you're having a bad day isn't valid, as if pain isn't or shouldn't be part of being human. Pain *is* part of being human. I read people all day and I'll say to them, "I can't take away your pain. This is what's coming, but you don't have to suffer. We have tools. We can work this; we can understand what's happening." But again, this does not take away the pain. I have every single tool and I went through a three-year depression. What was coming was coming. I knew there would be an end to it and that was the only thing I could count on to get me through.

It's Okay to Be Sad, Mad, or Glad

This message—positive vibes only—indicates that we should try to ignore pain; that negative emotions aren't valid. There is a word for a lack of emotions, it is *alexithymia*. I heard a podcast the other day and the topic of discussion was a study that had been done about human emotion. And the host asked, "How many words do you have for your emotions?"

And people replied, *happy*, *sad*, and *pissed*. That's it. We aren't armed with the proper vocabulary to express what we feel because we have been told our feelings aren't valid or they make us "soft."

We are so limited in our vocabulary of negative emotions because we've been told, "Put that away. That's not comfortable. Smile, everything's fine." I actually have a book called *The Emotions Thesaurus*, which I highly recommend. You can look up a primary emotion and then read all of it variants. My book, *The Seven Gates*, contains what I call "an emotion wheel." It's comprised of original emotions, and it branches out with the inclusion of other associated words. We need to get comfortable with unhappiness, with pain, with sorrow, and respect that these emotions are part of life.

It's like grief isn't allowed to be spiritual. "I'm so beyond; my vibration is so high that I don't feel." No, you're out of the body. You're dissociated and you're delusional is what you are. Today there's a toxic positivity movement. Movements are worrisome because sometimes they go the extreme. We don't want to be crying in every single street corner, but this movement *is* pushing us in the right direction by allowing us to accept grief, to accept sorrow.

As mentioned earlier, I have learned in my practice that people create situations so they can grieve their unlived and unexamined lives. For instance, I created cancer and divorce and losing my house and my hair. All of that was condoned, allowing me to become very depressed and to lay on a couch for three years. At the subconscious level, I was grieving the fact that I'd had a low vibration, not changing it before having children, and in general, having made a mess out of my life.

Grief is the most spiritual of emotions; unfortunately, we need a "reason" to grieve that is suitable for the world to approve of so that we can stay in bed. Saying that "I'm grieving my low level of consciousness and the chaos of a life I created" is not acceptable. I challenge you to not pay a high price like I did. Own the grief as you gain consciousness about your low vibrational thoughts and actions and grieve for as long as you need to.

I have to say that COVID has definitely brought issues of anxiety and worry and stress to the forefront. Having a mental health concern is a little bit more accepted now. And these uncomfortable emotions are increasingly talked about as a result. That's something positive that's come out of COVID—everything isn't great and shiny and bright and new.

Once you shatter the snow globe, forgive yourself for not knowing better. You will rebuild a real life, based on truth, higher consciousness, and you won't need to grieve. It seems harsh to say that I created my son's death, my job loss, or getting cancer, however, we create our reality based on our vibration, and when we are ready to make a major vibrational change, we need to grieve. In my opinion, grief is the highest vibration. It is the TI in the Law of Octaves, before the new level of consciousness begins at the new DO on the musical scale. (We will cover all of this in chapter 9, when we discuss the Law of Octaves.)

Defining Your Vibration

A cool exercise that demonstrates that every musical note has a frequency is to scatter some very fine sand over the head of a drum. Then take a tuning fork and strike a note just above the drumhead, causing it to vibrate. The sand should shift and assume a geometrical figure corresponding to the particular note that was played. When another note is sounded the sand will shift again and assume another figure. This shows that every vibration produces a corresponding geometric form.

A final example is the tuning fork, which is a forked-shaped metal object, usually made from aluminum or steel, which has two prongs. The prongs are set into vibration by hitting one with a rubber hammer. The prongs oscillate when activated due to the elastic properties of the material. The actual back-and-forth motion of the prongs is too small to see, however, the vibration of a prongs causes the air surrounding them to vibrate. The vibration in the air travels away as a sound wave that we hear when it causes our eardrums to vibrate.

Tuning forks are designed to produce a sound wave with a pure pitch (frequency). The tuning fork produces the musical note C at 512 vibrations per second. When I do chakra healings, I finish off with crystals, matching the color frequency of the chakra. I then strike the crystal with the tuning fork—almost creating a seal in the chakra—to maintain the proper vibration associated with that chakra.

The water studies done by Moroto Emoto are another example of this. Google *Moroto Emoto water consciousness* and you can see that negative thoughts and positive thoughts manifest as explicitly different images. Positive vibrations are great, and everyone wants to be happy, but the reality is that sometimes we're not. Accepting your shadow and accepting your negative emotions are a huge part of the spiritual process. Not doing so does not constitute a state of higher consciousness; it indicates denial and delusion on your part.

Examining Sticky Note Spirituality Buzzwords Related to the Principle of Vibration: "I eat only vegan and organic"

What's the real reason people eat only vegan and organic? There is a belief that if you eat vegan and organic you will vibrate at a higher frequency than if you eat fast-food or fried food. This idea comes from the ayurvedic concept of sattvic foods. Sattva is the highest vibration of the mind, and as such, it's associated with purity and cleanliness. Rajas is associated with activity and spicy hot food and tamas, the densest quality, is linked with inertia and low-quality food.

In Ayurveda there is a distinct link between food quality and your thoughts; the ancients understood that the third chakra is linked to the sixth chakra. The vagus nerve, which we have mentioned before but will elaborate on here, means "wanderer." It's the longest nerve in the body. It wanders through the body in such areas as the brain, stomach, intestines, liver, pancreas, and gallbladder. The vagus nerve links the third chakra, which is connected to the stomach and digestive system, with the sixth chakra, which is connected to the brain. Food quality is important, and if you're fortunate enough to be able to afford whole foods, organic foods, farm-to-table foods, please indulge. However, it is quite egotistical to believe that people who cannot afford organic juice or farm-to-table food are somewhat less spiritual.

The quality of the food contributes to the quality of your thoughts, as an assistant cleaning up your low-vibrational, putrefied thoughts of self-hatred, not the other way around. Ayurveda is a holistic mind-body-spirit health protocol. As quality food works your manas, your mind, they work your gut, they work your vibration, your thoughts, and your body. We have piecemealed this into thinking that vegan and organic somehow make us vibrate at a higher frequency, which is untrue.

We vibrate at the level of our thoughts.

It's How You Think, Not What You Eat

Your low-level consciousness produces a low-level vibration. You show up as a being with low-level consciousness and produce the results you call "life." You can do all of that drinking a ten-dollar green juice from Whole Foods and you will have the same outcome. You can eat fast-food, breath consciously, show compassion to your child rather than yell and scream, and those nuggets will do nothing to your vibration.

It's true that our food supply is horrible. Animals are abused, kept in horrendous conditions, and this frequency enters our body. However, it is overridden by the vibration of our thoughts. If you are on a spiritual path your choice of food can be the food that has a cleaner, higher vibration. This then supports the spiritual work that hopefully you're doing at the same time: that of changing your thoughts. Einstein said, "Everything is energy and that's all there is to it. Match the frequency of the reality you want and you cannot help but get that reality. It can be no other way. This is not philosophy. This is physics."

This vegan/organic trend has morphed into a big movement. Again, what's wrong with it? First of all, you have to be rich to go to Whole Foods, which tends to specialize in vegan and organic food. It's called "Whole Paycheck" for a reason! It's great if you can eat organic and vegan and drink ten-dollar juices every day, but that doesn't mean you're more spiritual than the average Joe. What are your thoughts? Tell me what you're thinking. I don't care so much about what you're eating, because again, the quality of your thoughts is going to eclipse the purity of the food and the drink.

Everything has a vibration and yes, there's prana; there's a life force in food. That's why the shamans of the day, when they were chasing the buffalo, would give ceremonial thanks to the buffalo before they took its life.

Often, we pray over our food, which helps to shift the vibration. If water changes its consciousness based on our prayer, why wouldn't we pray over food? Even if you're eating chicken nuggets, it's a nice practice. But really, it's your thoughts that count.

Like certain foods, alcohol contains a low vibration. Yes, it's toxic to the body, but one of the reasons it's of low vibration is because it's a coping mechanism for escapism, which is not adult, it's denial. It's delusion.

Therefore, if you're eating green and/or drinking green juice and you're still in a delusional state and you're not aware of what you're creating, don't waste the ten dollars on the juice! If you abstain from alcohol because you have an alcoholic parent, psychically you're no healthier than the alcoholic because you're thinking on the same vibrational wavelength.

Each one of you is in denial.

JUDGMENTS AND VALUES

People have an issue with medication as well but my guides say, "Earthly problems require earthly solutions." We have earthly tools like medication to help us. Negating the use of these tools and playing martyr and victim is another way to suffer, and another judgment. It's just like the person who refuses alimony. What you're trying to say is that you're strong and courageous. Again, those are states of mind, and that is just overcompensation. "I'm so strong, I don't need alimony." Or "I'm so strong, I don't need a pain med."

Just take the medicine. I'm not saying you have to; I'm just saying if you have those belief systems, know that they're not all true. Again, if they aren't universal truths, they're value statements and judgments. The state of mind, the vibration in which you're creating the value system around whole food, abundance, being spiritual, for instance, will determine your reality. If you cannot afford ten-dollar juice, the thought *I'm broke* will determine your inability to buy it.

Everyone has a value system. You may not be aware of what your values are, but that vibration of your values resonates in your subconscious and creates the realities of your life. Values themselves usually don't cause too many problems; it's the judgment associated with that value that's the problem.

For instance, if being a hard worker is a value statement, the judgment is that being lazy is bad or wrong. The judgment hasn't been integrated as a thought of a high vibration and thus it will create problems. You will beat yourself up for being "lazy," or not productive, or for taking a vacation. You will meet people in your life who are lazy because your subconscious is trying to integrate the lesson that there is a healthy vibration between hardworking and lazy and you need to find that vibration and operate from that place.

Again, I call this the 48 to 52: the midpoint between the values and judgments, or in this case, being efficient. *Positive vibes only* implies that negative thoughts, depressed feelings, and grief are judgments and as such are "bad."

How does your psyche reconcile this should you become heartbroken or lose a loved one?

CHAPTER 5

The Fourth Law— The Principle of Polarity

THIS LAW STATES, "Everything is dual. Everything has poles. Everything has its pair of opposites. Like and unlike are the same. Opposites are identical in nature, but different in degree. Extremes meet. All truths are but half-truths."

As children we learn things from our parents that we like and other things we dislike. Those things we dislike about our parents, for instance, drinking, yelling, lying, stealing, manipulating, become part of what I call "our bad buckets," which I touched on earlier. The bad buckets are the shadow aspects of our parents that we fail to integrate and as we mature they may cause problems in our lives.

If we see something in our parents we don't like or approve of, we tend to display the opposite behavior. If they drank, for instance, you may shun alcohol. If your mother wasn't clear or manipulated situations you might become hyper-focused on clarity and transparency. The Law of Polarity states that these are the same things. Opposites are the same. All truths are half-truths. What you do to oppose what your parent is doing is a half-truth because indeed you are exactly like your parent: same coin, different side.

Most people don't like to hear that one. "All paradoxes may be reconciled." You and the person you dislike are the same. You and your partner are the same. Your annoying, whiny kid is you; yes, you're an annoying whiny kid! Accept it and move on. What you don't like in another is what you don't like in yourself. And it is something that you have yet to reconcile and integrate.

Time to Look in the Mirror

One tenet of developing a spiritual practice is to determine who is pushing your buttons and what that's triggering in you. You will then know the qualities you need to work on within yourself. As we've learned, at the moment of conception, the issues your parents were dealing with within themselves became your subconscious programming. If they had an issue with their in-laws because they were pushy, you will become pushy. Your purpose was to meet your parent's unmet needs and mirror back to them their unintegrated shadow aspects.

In an ideal world, your parents would have identified your pushiness as something unintegrated in themselves and changed this before you turned fourteen. Then the pushiness would not have become a solidified personality trait of yours. However, it requires a very high level of consciousness to do this work, and it is rarely, if ever done. When you are fourteen you take on your own energetic karma and keep lugging your mother's and father's around, which interferes with your life's purpose.

If you become pushy and don't recognize it, you will tend to criticize pushy people. If you identify that this is your programming inherited at conception you can begin to integrate this quality and make the subconscious conscious. The Law of Polarity states all truths are but half-truths and opposites are equal. Again, doing the opposite of your parents is essentially doing the same thing. It is only in the midpoint, the 48 to 52 of the 0 to 100 scale, that we find balance, stability, and health. At this point behavior change becomes real and we no longer are affected by pushy people. Vibration has actually shifted via a higher consciousness.

My book *The Seven Gates* contains a seven-step model to reveal subconscious patterns. The second step is to ask yourself what you don't like about the person, place, thing, or situation that is presenting in your current situation. The answer is a mirror reflecting the answer back at you.

My book, *The Truth Is in the Triangle* contains a similar strategy for couples. If a "mistress" shows up in your relationship it is there to help you integrate something that you have failed to see or heal, yet see in others. A mistress is something that interrupts the relationship. It can be a real mistress, but it doesn't have to be. It might be a real addiction, a work schedule, traffic, a child. Again, this person, place, thing, or situation is showing up to mirror back to you the side of the coin you haven't acknowledged and integrated.

In my *Dethroning Olympus* workbook, I work with families to bring them to an understanding that their children are mirroring back to them unintegrated aspects of themselves. I say to parents, "Do your work so your children don't have to do it for you!" What you fail to recognize in yourself is passed on to your children as work they have to do to relieve and/or mitigate ancestral and transgenerational trauma.

This is also a polarity. If the pendulum keeps swinging robustly from right to left and back again because generation after generation doesn't address the extreme swings, the traumas of the family don't get resolved. Stopping the swinging and living in the 48 to 52 is the solution to healing these ancestral traumas and emotional loyalties.

EXAMINING STICKY NOTE SPIRITUALITY BUZZWORDS RELATED TO THE PRINCIPLE OF POLARITY: "I AM A LIGHTWORKER"

What's wrong with this phrase and how do we apply the Law of Polarity to it to truly understand its essence? As the law states, opposites meet. If you only desire to be a lightworker, you are denying your shadow. A spiritual path without the analysis of the shadow is a sham.

If there's light, there's dark, and that's all there is too it. Let's analyze this and let's look at how the subconscious works in so doing. As I've mentioned before, growing up you made judgments about the good and bad qualities (the "good and bad buckets") that your parents had. The good qualities, the light, were qualities that caused no problems in your psyche and you embraced them fully. The bad qualities, or dark aspects, however, posed a problem, causing your inner voice to judge and criticize yourself, often creating self-destructive patterns in your life.

When you say, "I am a lightworker," you're on one side of the pendulum, let's say the 100. Here you're negating the bad buckets, and this perpetuates subconscious trauma. Most people try and live in the light and own their good qualities, however, inevitably the shadow aspects must surface.

As the law states, the swing to the right is equal to the swing to the left.

Everything is Reflecting *You!*

I once had a client who was being very rigid with her spending (on the 0 to 100 scale, she was at a 0; that's how extreme her behavior was. After a few weeks of not spending any money on anything but the essentials, she called me for a session because her cat was sick and hadn't eaten in days. When I opened the Akashic Records, the cat showed me that he was wearing a straitjacket. I removed it from him and the woman screamed at me, "What did you just do, he just ran to the food bowl and began to eat!"

The pendulum had swung to the left so she had to spend money on my services and the veterinarian, actions that swung her pendulum to the other extreme of 100. We decided that instead of being so tight with her money she would indulge once a week, which would help to alleviate the pendulum swings.

In looking at the subconscious pattern she was being loyal to she spoke about her father. He had implored her to save money while he himself had been embezzling funds from his employer, landing him in jail. She was working with the subconscious mind, the thoughts of which she had inherited at conception, which reflected a low level of consciousness. By permitting herself to spend a little money each week she was stopping the swing of the pendulum and raising her consciousness level around her finances.

If you're giving messages to or doing healing on people and you're not seeing that it's a reflection of you, you're missing the mark. In fact, you're way *off* the mark. If there was no light, nothing would cast a shadow. Jung said, "The cave you fear to enter holds your gold."

I'm a shadow worker, not a lightworker. Do your work.

THE SHADOW SIDE OF THE LIGHT

Listen to the extremes that are articulated in people's speech. Saying one is a lightworker implies that they also have a lot of darkness. *Negredo* is a Latin word for "black" or "dark," as employed in a term like *dark night of the soul.* Its image is a very famous one that represents this dark side of the human psyche. You actually come to wholeness with yourself when you explore the Negredo by doing your shadow work; when you look at your darkness; when you look at what you don't like about yourself; when you allow your enemy to be a mirror of yourself; when someone annoys you—and you integrate all of that. That's being a true lightworker.

Look at what you came in to deal with in this lifetime. Are you going to tell me you are all light and bright? No. You have judgments. Saying "positive vibes only" is a judgment. I say judgments are confessions. People who say they're lightworkers can be the darkest of the dark. If this is you, you just may be afraid of your darkest thoughts and would rather not believe you're capable of what you're capable of.

Most people who spend their life saying, "I'm a lightworker" and "positive vibes only" and "I vibrate so high" are so afraid of the dark because they're drawn to it. They may have had a past life where they were a priestess, or they were some witch and practiced black magic or sorcery. If you believe in that, read my book *Witch Bitch* where I talk about these things. If you're drawn to the dark, it's hard to toe the line of the light. Instead, you deny and you are deluded. "I'm light and bright," and I call "bull." Healers need to heal themselves, not others. If I pretend that I heal anybody, I'm a narcissist and a hypocrite. I heal absolutely nobody.

May I tell you truths that you're not capable of telling yourself because you're scared? Absolutely. May I shine some light on something that you're not 100 percent clear about and that you probably know but don't want to admit? Maybe. But the idea that your work as a lightworker to heal anyone is absurd. You heal yourself. And the only reason you're doing lightwork or healing work or intuitive work is to heal yourself. Do not think there's anything more to it. Always remember that the advice you gave is the advice you need.

This is the Negredo. It is the first stage in the individuation process. It happens alone, in the dark, and is often accompanied by grief and loneliness.

In shamanism, the Negredo represents the direction of the West, the dark night of the soul, Saturn cycles, and the transmutation of lead to gold in alchemy. But first comes the decomposition of what you used to be, to make room for what you'll become. In the image above there are two people, the duality of what you think you are. The process is to create unity within. This union is symbolized by the mystical marriage, the *Heiros Gamos*, where you marry your masculine and feminine aspects, spirit and matter, and higher and lower consciousness.

Examining Sticky Note Spirituality Buzzwords Related to the Principle of Polarity: "Everything will be okay"

What's wrong with this phrase and why is it used so frequently in our culture? And how does the Principle of Polarity apply to it? There is a common desire to pretend that spirituality, engaging in ceremony and ritual, and/or adorning oneself with the accoutrements and lessons of a new age practice will be a panacea to the trials of life. That's delusion—another swing of the pendulum. Just because you work with Spirit; have knowledge of the universal laws; channel, meditate, or read tarot cards, you're still susceptible to the pain of life. If you're only living in a mindset of "everything will be okay" you're going to get hit extra hard when the pendulum swings in the opposite direction. Similar to being a lightworker, you're only seeing one side of the coin.

What's wrong with this message then, that "Everything will be okay." Yes, it will be okay but like I said before, I can't take away your pain. I am a believer that certain things are determined. Certain things are going to happen to you. Some transit, some cycle, will dictate this. What's important is not that this is happening, it's how you choose to experience it and the level of consciousness you choose to experience it with. And nobody gets to determine your level of consciousness but you.

All that said, I'm also a believer in free will. I have twin boys and I often get the question, If they have the same chart, do they have the same life? The answer is no. They're each individual, with different ways of living out their chart. Their thread is the same because they were conceived at the same time. However, they get to decide *how* to live the story out. What myth will they embody and how they play out that myth is determined by their free will and level of consciousness.

When one of them undergoes a new cycle, for example moon conjunct Mars, the other has the same cycle. That's the cycle that started when I was diagnosed with breast cancer for a third time. They each lived it out a different way. They choose the vibrational level at which to respond. They choose the level of consciousness at which to respond.

How many other people had a moon in Sagittarius when Mars went into Sagittarius that same day? Millions of people! Does that mean all of their mothers got cancer? No. The creation myth, your life, and how you play it out determines what happens, the story you tell when you are visited by that transit. How you deal with what may be difficult events and the level of consciousness that you embody in so doing is the difference between pain and suffering.

Pain and Suffering

Haruki Murakami, a Japanese writer, adopted and often proclaimed an old Buddhist maxim, "Suffering is not part of life, we do it to ourselves." And I absolutely agree! I'm a Pisces. Pisces love to suffer. We are the scapegoat. We're the martyr, we're the rescuer. We are dramatic. Pin us to the cross; we love our suffering. Everyone has Pisces and Neptune somewhere in their chart, so somewhere, somehow, we inflict suffering on ourselves.

Pain is different.

There are two types of people. There are people that are more drawn to pain like I am, and those that more drawn to pleasure. Same coin, different side. We've just established that everything has a polarity or another side. But both sides represent the same thing. People who seek hedonism are in pain, and people who are in pain might actually derive some kind of secret pleasure from experiencing that pain. That's called suffering.

When you choose to suffer beyond the pain, that is a choice and you may like it. It may be pleasure for you. And you know who you are! If you happen to have a lot of water in your chart, or little water, oftentimes you like to suffer. These are polarities. In Buddhism there are four noble truths and Buddha does use the word *suffer*. I'd like to substitute it with *pain*, or *the truth of suffering, the truth of the cause of suffering, the truth of the end of suffering*, and *the truth of the path that leads to end of suffering*. You cannot eliminate pain because as mentioned earlier you are limited, a) by your body, b) by the physical plane that we inhabit, c) by your wheel and d) fourth, by your cross.

You are limited all around. That's why there are four doors to the Shri Yantra. That's why there are four entryways in the zodiac. That's why there are four stages of alchemy and four directions in shamanism. And four is a number of death, because it relates to limitation; it relates to this earthly body and this earthly plane.

The Cyclical Nature of Life

We are just a series of cycles. We all start off at the lowest level of consciousness (the consciousness of our parents at the moment of conception). We are constantly going upward through our cycles—and cycles are always spiraling upward, always! We repeat the same cycle over and over, as we will with Jupiter every twelve years, as we will with Mars every two years, as we will with the sun every year. It's always in an upward direction because it's always in hopes of taking you to a level of consciousness that's higher than the original cycle, which began with your creation/conception.

Now if you've started off at a very high level of consciousness, good for you! Perhaps your parents conceived you with a high level of consciousness. Therefore, you're ahead of the game. However, the process is the same for everyone—to raise consciousness to the next level—in which case you don't have to keep repeating certain things throughout your life. The seasons show us this; every winter is followed by a spring.

Nobody is going to be in a Negredo or in a dark night of the soul where there isn't a spring afterward and a rebirth. It's impossible because this is the cycle of the larger universe. It's the cycle of nature. Therefore, it's the cycle of the human being.

The astrological wheel is a circle. We are constantly going through the wheel over and over and over again. We start at the first house, which is the birth so to speak, the initiation. We go all year around our sun until our birthday when things come full circle again. We're constantly in a cycle.

This is represented by the medicine wheel in shamanism. Again, it's a wheel with a cross because we are limited by nature, we're limited by the body, we're limited by the earthly plane, we're limited by all of the things of this plane. Therefore, it's represented by a circle with the four directions. These are the stages of alchemy: The Rubedo, the Negredo, the Albedo, and the Citrinitas.

Then there are the chakras. We are constantly going from the bottom chakra, the first chakra, all the way up to the seventh. And they're cyclical too. Once you reach that glimmer of happily ever after, or the transcendence you might feel for half a second as you're in the seventh chakra, you're back to the first chakra to do it all over again and to raise your vibration in so doing. In Kabbalah, the Tree of Life is another way of expressing this.

With the Sephiroth are the ten circles of the Tree of Life in Kabballah. It is a hierarchical representation of how we grow in consciousness as we make our way up the tree. The top circle, or crown, is Kether. Immediately below it is a dotted line representing our fall from grace, like Adam's fall from Eden. Once we incarnate, we immediately have a fall, because we are expelled from the universal womb into the maternal womb. The bottom sephirot is Malkuth. Once we fall out of heaven—the crown, Kether, the highest level of consciousness—we start at the bottom, at Malkuth, which is similar to the first chakra.

We travel through all of these circles and then we repeat it. That's the good news. If we understood cycles, we could really maximize growth. As I mentioned earlier but bears repeating here, in 2009 I had Jupiter conjunct Jupiter in the second house. This brought me love, a great job, money, my dissertation, a Ph.D., and a position of authority in the college where I was dean of nursing.

Now, twelve years later (remember, a Jupiter cycle is twelve years long) I have that same cycle, which means that threads from twelve years ago will resurface in a growth pattern. This follows the Fibonacci Sequence in nature. The Fibonacci Sequence is a series of numbers derived from classical mathematics that are applicable to the fields of advanced mathematics, nature, statistics, and computer science.

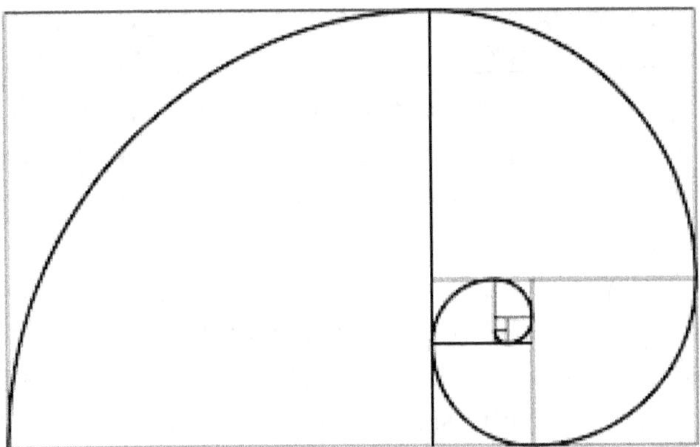

The Fibonacci Sequence Spiral

MAPPING YOUR CYCLES

If you trace your cycles from childhood, you will know exactly what is coming and how to use the energy that ensues. I knew in nature that winter is followed by spring. I also knew that my Jupiter cycle was my "spring" and would occur twelve years to the day from my last one. Ages associated with Jupiter cycles are 12, 24, 36, 48, 60, 72, 84, 96, and 108. One hundred eight is the number of beads on a mala, which are prayer beads in Eastern traditions. They represent the amount of spiritual growth we have programmed in our soul.

This does not mean that I didn't get depressed or feel suicidal when I was in a Saturn transit. Why not? Again, because I knew spring was coming. With Jupiter, growth must occur as it does in the Fibonacci spiral. You decide how big the spiral gets. With Saturn you will have skinny cows, lean years inevitably—and you will decide how you will live them out.

Every cycle we take around the zodiac is intended to raise our consciousness. Everybody's aging. From the moment you were born, you're aging. Now you might use skin cream, you might eat well, you might exercise, you might do karate, you might go in for plastic surgery but your number of years are still your numbers of years.

If you're sixty and you look decrepit, or sixty and you look great, that's on you. That's down to your free will. Spirituality works the same way; every single person is moving upward and onward. This is not reserved for privileged people. This is not reserved for people with crystals or people doing chakra work and Reiki. We are all in cycles that move onward and upward.

Are you going to keep repeating that same level of consciousness every time that cycle appears? Just like you choose to age wisely and age better, you also can stumble and stumble and stumble and stumble and stumble 'till you're fifty, sixty, seventy years old. Finally, at that point, you might say, "Oh, maybe I should do things differently." Just remember that the cycles are here to help you; they're working in your favor to help you achieve a higher state of consciousness, always and forever.

CHAPTER 6

The Fifth Law— The Principle of Rhythm

THIS FIFTH LAW STATES, "Everything flows out and in. Everything has its tides. All things rise and fall. The pendulum swings, manifesting everything. The measure of the swing to the right is the measure of the swing to the left. Rhythm compensates."

Life has a rhythm. This law refers to that rhythm. We see this rhythm in, for instance, the tides four times per day, the moon cycles every twenty-nine days, the four seasons each year, and the planets orbiting in the solar system. The rhythm of life is circular, and the point of tension of that circle is called an opposition; the pendulum will swing from right to left, from one extreme to the other.

My favorite analogy is the moon. On the new moon start something new, for example a diet. Seven days in you will have your first "crisis"—perhaps you'll start craving a cupcake. By the fourteenth day, you will be at the full moon. At this point you'll have an opposition—a complete pendulum swing from when you started the diet on the new moon and that "crisis" you had at day seven. This will become a scream to change direction. Either abandon the diet completely or cheat by eating the pizza you've been craving or, alternatively, start that gym routine you've been putting off. Depending on your will, something must change!

By the time another seven days has gone by, the desire to cheat will have subsided a little, albeit you will still have another small crisis. About seven days later a new moon will appear once again and you can start something new once again. Because the moon is the luminary that goes around the sun the most quickly every twenty-nine days, it's easy to see the Principle of Rhythm in this metaphor.

This same thing happens with every other planet. If you track the cycles of Jupiter, you will have the opposition at six years. If you track Saturn, you'll have the opposition at fourteen years. These cycles of the planets are one indicator of this universal principle. Astrology speaks to the concept of opposition beautifully.

In astrology, when two planets are in opposition, they create conflict in your outside world. These two planetary archetypes are in your subconscious, unintegrated shadow, or your bad buckets, and you create a situation around them in your real life to help you reconcile your subconscious programming. When two planets are in opposition, I call these "the competitive voices." The competitive voices exist to make you realize you are swinging either too far to the left or to the right; the answer is in the 48 to 52, in the midpoint.

Equanimity, as I've mentioned before, is a favorite word of mine from the enneagram literature—it's an attempt to be balanced, to achieve the 48 to 52. Most spiritual traditions posit that there is only one real illness, that of imbalance. I understand from my study of the moon phases that not everyone has the same version of 48 to 52, but achieving whatever definition of balance or midpoint works for you is the place where the swinging pendulum stops. In astrology, when two planets have a planetary conjunction, in a set amount of time afterward they reach an opposition.

And depending on the speed of the planet, the opposition might happen at various times. For instance, Mars has a two-year cycle around the sun so the opposition would occur at one year. If you look back at what you started at the conjunction of the two planets, the opposition, the polarity swing (0 to 100), has reached its peak point of tension. The planet must keep moving so you are forced as a result to make a choice and make a change.

The universe provides solutions for this swing of the extremes; I call them "neutralizers." Neutralizers are specific times in your life when, if you pay attention to the other principles, you can slow the swing and achieve equanimity or self-mastery, the 48 to 52.

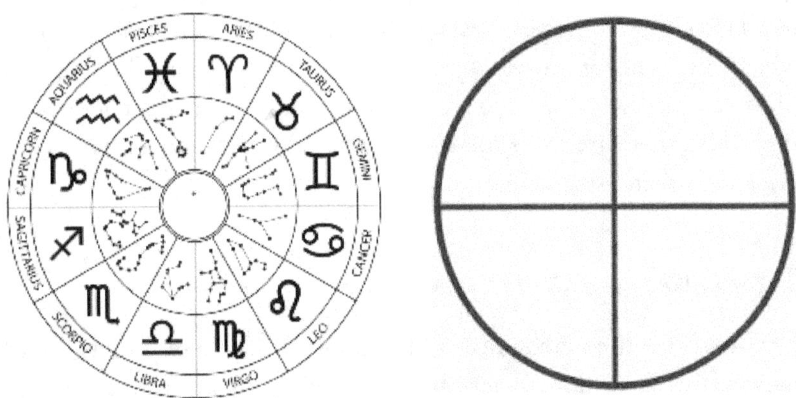

On the left, an astrological wheel and on the right, the medicine wheel used in shamanism. It reveals the four directions used in shamanic practice.

As we know, the astrological wheel is circular. The sun (every 365 days), as all planets do (with their respective speeds), go around the zodiac every year (sun) to 264 years (Pluto). The medicine wheel is used in shamanism to indicate the four cardinal directions. Each direction is representative of our spiritual journey; we "walk" the wheel throughout life as we grow spiritually. Each direction is represented by a lesson and an animal totem.

EXAMINING STICKY NOTE SPIRITUALITY BUZZWORDS RELATED TO THE PRINCIPLE OF RHYTHM: "BEING NOT DOING."

This is a wonderful concept to deconstruct because there is so much to work with here. But what does it really mean and how does it correspond to the Principle of Rhythm? There are a lot of people who say,

"I'm going to be in a state of *being*; I'm not going to *do* anything." But being and doing work together. Like so much of what we've discussed in this book, they're complementary forces.

This notion of being in a state of being goes back to the idea that the universe will provide. But, again, this is very innocent thinking, very limited thinking. It's very entitled to think that you're just going to be and things are going to manifest in your lap. You have to balance these energies. Yes, you have to be and that's the 48 to 52 where there's equanimity and you're in a state of balance. But you also need action! There is a time for rest and there is a time for action. In Ayurveda, there are three mental energies: the mahagunas, which are tamas, rajas, and sattva.

Tamas, Rajas, and Sattva

Let's examine the mahagunas a little more closely here. Tamas is like inertia. You can call it laziness, but we're just speaking from an energy perspective now. It's inertia. Let's just for a second call it "being." I'm not saying it's equivalent, but just so you can understand the concept let's call it "being" for the moment.

Rajas is the passion, the go-getter, the part of you that penetrates life. Rajas is the quality of passion, activity, drive, momentum, and dynamism a person has to have in order to make things happen. Rajas can be fueled by passion and desire and can be increased by eating fiery foods, bodybuilding, and running or talking loudly and engaging in competition.

The great mythologist Joseph Campbell had another word for this rajas energy: *the call*, which is the first step of a hero's twelve-step journey. Its dictates are rooted in ancient wisdom, primarily astrology. When two planets connect, they're inviting you to become something more than what you currently are. It's important that you step up at this time, for if you don't, you may be missing something big. Campbell said, in *A Hero with a Thousand Faces*, "Refusal of the call converts its adventure into its negative. Walled in boredom, hard work or 'culture.' The subject loses the power of significant affirmative action and becomes a victim to be saved." The lunar cycle is the easiest to "see" since it occurs every twenty-nine and a half days. Set an intention on the new moon, don't follow through, and see what happens at the full moon fourteen days later. This is tamas.

In astrology, all transiting conjunctions are initiations. All conjunctions deserve an intention, something that you do, that you move, that you penetrate, that you push into the world. You're not supposed to be still at a conjunction. You need your rajasic energy, which makes things happen for you.

In nature the butterfly and the chickee die if they are helped in pushing themselves out of their cocoon or the egg. As they struggle to emerge, they are building strength in their wings and their beak, which will allow them to fly and eat as they mature. To believe that we don't need to push through, or penetrate life at times, is again infantile. Plant the seeds with action steps, then reap what you sow, with being.

Cycles and rhythmic patterns of growth require being *and* doing; a time of rest and a time of action. The principle of being harbors an understanding that this too shall pass. You can *be*, once you're done *doing*.

Oftentimes, being is reserved for difficult times when you may need to sit still. This is the wrong time to act and be rajasic. This is where people tend to get very distracted; they get very busy instead of sitting still, as they ought to do. They don't want to sit still, because they don't want to do the inner work, they don't want to go within. But this is exactly what you need to do at this time.

When you're in Negredo, when you're in a dark night of the soul, when you're in a Saturn transit, those are times to pause, to stop, to just be. If you overdo something you're going to crash at the equivalent level. When you are getting the backlash of something in your life, this is the pendulum at the other extreme of its swing and you have brought it there.

When two planets are in a conjunction, they basically meet eye to eye. This energy is similar to that of a new moon. It's the origin and time to start something. If you fail to utilize the energy when the two planets are in opposition, you will have the fallout for failing to use the energy. Mars is the energy of a warrior. It is the impulse, creator energy that motivates us to action.

If at a Mars cycle you show up lazy and disinterested, then one year later at the opposition you will endure a crisis from this failure to act. The universe is always leading us in the right direction for our soul's growth, but how often we lose out on these opportunities! This is a microcosm of what happens when you miss out on bigger "calls to action," usually out of fear.

Okay, enough about tamas and rajas, let's talk about sattva. Sattva is that perfect balance, and is often described as purity, balance, and harmony. Sattva is calmness, contentment, goodness, and purity. It is believed that sattva qualities are linked to meditation and the attainment of enlightenment. Sattvic foods are whole foods and fresh foods.

Working *with* the Planetary Energies

We need all three of these energies, which move cyclically. You can't just think that you're going to be in a state of being. That's like saying I'm going to inhale and never exhale. With the cycling of these three energies in our lives, we see how a sense of rhythm is created. Our job is to recognize when each particular energy is called for.

Understanding planetary forces also gives us the tools we need to respond properly. During my first divorce my husband was coming at me with a sword and I was fighting back with a butter knife. The Old Testament dictates "an eye for an eye." This does not mean revenge; this means that you should retaliate with the same force as someone coming at you. Fight fair, not stupid. I was wearing a nice-guy mask and retaliating with an unequal weapon, when I too should have been using a sword. A nice-guy mask is simply an innocent archetype, reflecting a desire to remain in victim mode and be saved. I was not a victim, but in fear of not honoring the cult leader and appearing fierce, I played small and paid a high price.

Understanding the planetary energies can help you with a plan of action. With a Mars cycle, you show up like a warrior. With a Saturn cycle you show up slow and steady, with boundaries and cautious. With a Venus cycle you show up with grace and elegance.

In chapter 2, verse 31 of the Bhagavad Gita, Krishna states to Arjuna, the warrior and protagonist of the story, "There is nothing more auspicious for a warrior than a righteous war. If you will not fight this righteous war, then you will fail in your duty, lose your reputation and incur sin." We are so often called to action and rather than showing up as our soul intended, we cower under the weight of what the world might think. These may be predetermined values that we don't subscribe to anymore.

In the Gospel of Thomas in the Gnostic Gospels, Jesus said, "If you do not fast from the world, you will not find the Kingdom." He did not mean literally fast or run away to an ashram. He meant fast from the thoughts of others, especially the voices in your head, which are your parents' voices egging you on to live their unlived lives.

Thus, we are granted opportunities with these planetary cycles and universal laws, and we waste them. When the opposition occurs, one, five, or ten years later, we blame our situation on such things as a car accident, getting fired, or going through a divorce. If you go back to the origin story, the moment of the planetary conjunction, and see that you failed to heed the call, the opposition is simply mirroring that failure to act.

The thing with oppositions—and this is what's super important, because they're externalized—is that when they occur it feels like someone is doing something *to you*. But in reality, this is an opportunity not only for you to learn equanimity and find a midpoint, but to use that person who's involved in the scenario as a mirror because whatever they're doing to you is what you do to you.

For example, if your sister bullies you it's because you bully yourself. You can realize this in an internal dialogue when you look at the oppositions in your chart. Oppositions are opportunities because you get a mirror and you get an opportunity to see the midpoint, and to achieve equanimity.

SEARCHING FOR SQUARES AND OPPOSITIONS

How do we stop the extremes from happening; how do we balance ourselves? How do we get to this state of self-mastery? Go to your chart and find every opposition. Find every opposition and find the midpoint. Again, oppositions are opportunities. In your chart, if you have two planets that are directly opposite one another, there's a midpoint by sign; by house. And if you find that then you can see exactly where it is that you need to meet in the middle. You can see that in your chart and you can see what opportunities you have for equanimity because the oppositions are automatically creating rhythms in your life.

This is the Principle of Rhythm in action. You cannot avoid it, because your level of consciousness is not that high.

Oppositions are the best opportunities for one to learn and grow and squares are the other hard aspects that do this for us too. So, as with oppositions, go to every square in your chart and find the midpoint. That's the point of self-mastery. We are all given some "baggage" at the moment of conception that we must work through. In Hinduism it is called *sanchitta karma*, the sum of one's past karmas. In this lifetime we get a small percentage of that karma to work through, called *prarabdha karma*.

In Greek mythology, the Fates, specifically Clotho, spin the thread of human life for this lifetime, a few days after conception. These two instances refer to the issue we incarnated with in order to work through in this lifetime. Notice I said "issue." We only have one issue woven through our conception story all the way to our death. I call this our creation myth, and it follows us through life, in every situation that troubles us.

A human being cannot tackle more than one issue in a lifetime. When I counsel clients, I can identify the myth that they're living. The situation they present with always goes back to that myth, that moment of conception, that prarabdha karma, and Clotho weaving your life on one thread. On your astrological chart, you can see the karma in the form of squares and oppositions. Those situations will repeat over and over again so that you can master the lesson they are trying to teach you.

Another way to understand your issue is to identify what crisis happened to you before you turned seven. This was the first crack in the system, and you're trying to repair it by becoming "not that" in every situation. This links back to your bad bucket items and even determines the illnesses you have. Like Arjuna was trying to do, we don't want to fight the fight we came to fight in this lifetime so all too often we cop out and refuse to step up to work on our own spiritual growth.

We waste time pretending to be victims, saviors, and rescuers for others. We don't do the inner work and then complain when the world is unfair and things don't work out our way. When you get a job it comes with a job description, however, when our soul has a job, we fail to honor its job description.

Every opposition midpoint and every square midpoint presents an opportunity to master in this lifetime. Many people ask me their purpose. That's your purpose—*you* are your purpose. The most important words ever written at the Temple of Apollo at Delphi are "know thyself" and "nothing in excess." Still, most of us do not know ourselves, and we are swinging from 0 to 100 like the pendulum, which is excess. Remember, even scarcity is excess.

The 48 to 52 is the only midpoint. Understanding squares and oppositions are a great way to know oneself because they are crisis points in the psyche, and the midpoint between the two planets is the answer to your crisis. Self-mastery can occur only when you know your mind and achieve equanimity between the extremes.

In mythology Chiron the centaur, who is associated with self-mastery, rules the master gland. This is the pituitary gland and it's linked to the primordial wound in this lifetime: the one issue that's threaded throughout your life. Chiron's orbit around the sun is 48 to 52 years. This is not a coincidence. When Chiron returns "home" to his natal placement, you are equipped with the key to truly master yourself.

Mythologically speaking, Chiron's favorite student was Hercules. Hercules accidentally hit Chiron in his thigh with an arrow dipped in Hydra's blood, which would never heal. Chiron went around the world for 48 to 52 years looking for someone to help him but no one could. He had to heal himself upon his return home.

Like Chiron, we waste so much time deviating from our path in search of a savior or a knight in shining armor, images which are in our collective unconscious. However, *you* are your savior, and *you* are your knight in shining armor.

You Are Your Purpose

Save yourself. Again, *that's* your purpose. Upon Chiron's return home he realized he had agency and negotiated with Zeus and found the answer to his problem. The answers were within him always, but until achieving the midpoint, the 48 to 52, and returning home to himself, he couldn't heal or have self-mastery. He was the original *wounded warrior*— a term that we use today to refer to those who heal others but who never seem to have the antidote to their own problems. Your only real job on this planet is to try not to miss the mark so badly that you burn—by flying as Icarus did—too close to the sun. *Every single person* is entitled to do this work when they're here (in a body, living on planet Earth). I call this the wounded ruler archetype, where we own our divinity through our humanity. *Everyone* has the Divine within them and everyone is held to these laws whether they know it or not.

By knowing these laws, you can make them work for you. As a result, your highs are not too high and your lows are not too low. The closer we get to that 48 to 52, the closer we get to that balance.

The pendulum swinging from 0 to 100, with our desired range in the middle.

From the age of seven on, we have "neutralizers" to teach us how to balance the swings and achieve the 48 to 52 midpoint of self-mastery, but we rarely pay attention. The pendulum will swing 0 to 100 until you decide to change. You will get an opportunity every seven years to achieve a midpoint. If you do not take the opportunity, the swings will continue.

I had a client the other day who shared with me how he felt about his significant other. "I love this woman. She's my soulmate," he told me. And basically, he's in a codependent addictive relationship wherein he was experiencing a high that he had never achieved before. And that's wonderful if you get to experience that once in your life or twice or three times; lucky you. But know that that is not sustainable. That swing of the pendulum is not sustainable and not maintainable. It's also not healthy. Many coupled individuals I see in my practice complain that the passion has gone out of their marriage, or that they're not head over heels in love with their partner anymore.

That's part of the self-mastery. In relationships, part of the self-mastery is to meet our own needs while we share a life, or what I call "a thread," together. Hopefully the highs and lows are eliminated over time as you live and grow with this person who is your partner.

Now, some people live in that and think they thrive in living out the extremes every day. They're chaotic, they're violent, they have sex swinging from the chandeliers. There's a lot of drama in their lives. That's not self-mastery. Good for you if you want that, and why not? Just know that that isn't the law and it will not get you to self-mastery.

So, to wrap up, self-mastery is identifying the middle ground or being equanimous; not super, super high, not super, super low. I'm not saying that you shouldn't overdo anything. Obviously, you *feel*. We want to feel. That's a wonderful part of being human and we embrace it. But we don't embrace going to these major extremes day in and day out.

CHAPTER 7

The Sixth Law— The Principle of Cause and Effect

THIS LAW, the Principle of Cause and Effect, states, "Every cause has its effect. Every effect has its cause. Everything happens according to law. Chance is but a name for law not recognized. There are many planes of causation, but nothing escapes the law. Nothing happens by accident."

Everything happens for a reason. I dislike that statement, but it's true. In essence, that's what this law is about. There is a law that governs what's happening. You may not know the law because it may be happening at a high plane, then again, you're not deserving of that information. Accept your limitations but know that there is a reason for the reason.

Ralph Waldo Emerson said the Law of Cause and Effect is the "law of laws." All actions have reactions. What you initiate has consequences and will return back to its point of origin. All paths have an origin story and from that a chain reaction of events occurs. What determines the effects of your actions?

It Begins and Ends with Consciousness

It's all linked back to consciousness. If you enter into a behavior with conscious action, you will get that in return. Unconsciousness around a situation that you initiated does not keep you from the consequences of what you initiated. When you are conceived, the level of consciousness at which you were conceived started a chain reaction for the next nine months of your mother's pregnancy and then on into your lifetime. Everything in your lifetime is a result of that one moment in time when you inherited your conception story. And this is dictated by your previous karma.

As you grow and gain consciousness you can change the result of what happens as a result of your actions, if you change your level of consciousness. However, you can never change the origin story that began at the moment of conception. This is the thread of your lifetime. You're the product of the sexual contact of your parents.

The myth of Odysseus in Homer's *Odyssey* is a perfect representation of this example. Odysseus is gone for ten years to war and as a result it takes him ten years to return home. When he encounters his wife twenty years later, they're in the marital bedroom rearranging furniture and he says, "You cannot separate the olive branch from the marital bed." The bed post was made from the olive branch that was coming out of the floor. This illustrates the point that everyone is a product of their parents, good and bad, and you cannot remove your parents and their influence from your story or your psyche. Therefore, their level of consciousness is dictating all of your future behaviors, hence the results of your life when you live from an unconscious state and take no responsibility for anything until you decide to change.

As mentioned earlier, many years ago I was about to leave my first marriage and I heard a voice say, "take personal responsibility." This became my mantra for the next twenty years. I mistook the message to mean that I should blame myself for everything that I was going through, however, it was simply an invitation to change. I recognize now, because of this law, that I am responsible for how I react to everything that happens to me and that my state of consciousness created it. But, because of this law, I also learned to not take things personally.

I went through a three-year depression during a severe Pluto transit and lost my marriage, my house, my hair, and my financial and emotional stability. When I understood this law, I understood the cosmos. Pluto was going through Capricorn in 2020 as a result of having gone through Cancer more than one hundred and fifty years ago (the Law of Rhythm). This had nothing to do with me. However, the way I reacted to it was my responsibility.

The universe is vast, the cosmos are huge, and you cannot be held responsible for planetary movements. But what started with a planetary configuration, your reaction to it and how you handle it, at what level of consciousness you handle it at, is your responsibility and the "effect" of this law.

The Significance of Karma

The Law of Cause and Effect is also known as karma. *Karma* is a Sanskrit word meaning "action." The word first appeared in the Upanishads and then in the Vedas. For Hindus, karma is believed to govern all consciousness.

Karma is not fated but is determined by our actions, which operate according to our free will. I believe that in a deterministic world certain things will happen as a result of the limitations of being in the body, however, we also have free will which is my permission to respond according to my level of consciousness. We are exactly where we deserve to be in life. From our past actions, our current life, in part, is constructed.

Consciously choosing to do things differently is called "transmutation."

There's a big difference between transformation and transmutation. Transformation is when you stop and think about making a choice. Transmutation is when you own the choice you have made. Transmutation is not a change in behavior—it's a change in a belief system. We generate a conscious thought(s), we make high-vibrational choices, and we start seeing things shift. This occurs when we "own" this new level of consciousness and the new thought becomes automatic.

I used to bite my nails. When I realized this, I consciously decided not to bite them anymore, and I didn't. I haven't bitten my nails in over thirty years. I don't think about this now. This is transmutation. In the same way, spiritual growth may be the result of making your unconscious behaviors conscious, which then leads to positive change.

You earned your level of consciousness from previous karma built in previous lifetimes. If you choose free will and show up differently, that's transmutation. When that new spiritual belief, behavior, and practice becomes your way of life, you've transmuted—and therefore burned—karma. Everything we have ever thought or done contributes to our karma and is stored in the Akashic Records. When I read the records, I am reading the energy pattern of a person's soul from this life and past lives.

The energy pattern created is rooted in patterns of the Law of Cause and Effect, which dictate the probability of behavior and what the reaction will be. There are various types of karma, some that rebound in future lifetimes or those called "kriya mana," which are direct results of actions in this lifetime.

In certain philosophies, it is believed that difficult lifetimes have a direct relationship to past actions in past lives. In Indian philosophy, these are called samskaras. They are mental impressions or a psychological blueprint from past lives and the moment of conception in this lifetime.

When I read the Akashic Records I am reading the samskaras. Samskaras are the basis of karmic philosophy. Buddhists describe samskaras as "formations" and indeed they are formations in the energy field or the Akashic Records. In astrology, some people have a lot of squares and oppositions that cause a more difficult lifetime, while others have many trines and sextiles, which make for an easier time. However, in alchemy, Saturn is the planet of karma and everyone has Saturn somewhere in their natal chart and will experience transits and returns of Saturn too.

Examining Sticky Note Spirituality Buzzwords Related to the Principle of Cause and Effect: "Co-creating with God"

What's wrong with this buzz phrase *Co-creating with God?* And how does it relate to the Principle of Cause and Effect? *Everything* has to do with consciousness and creating has to do with the level of consciousness something is created at. This is the importance of conjunctions in the chart. When you start something, yes, you're co-creating with the universe, but you have to put your part into place.

What's in Your Subconscious?

You're creating something at a level of consciousness and that level of consciousness emanates from your subconscious. And if your subconscious is behaving from a place of violence, aggression, anger, unhealed wounds, scarcity—I don't care how conscious you are and how many ceremonies you participate in and how many candles you burn, and how much incense you light, you're creating with your subconscious god, which is a god of low-level consciousness.

"Man know thyself, and you will know the wonders of the universe" is written at the Oracle of Delphi in Greece. That's the secret: man know thyself. Healing myself is all about knowing myself. So yes, you co-create with God but what God does not determine is the level of consciousness at which you're creating and to what subconscious god you are being loyal. You can't blame God. *Your* level of consciousness is determining your life. So, if you attract a relationship, you created it, you brought it forth, and yes maybe God brought you together by destiny but you created the level of consciousness at which that relationship was built. You have agency and you have to take responsibility for that agency.

All that said, you can't see the level of consciousness in the astrological chart, ever. When I give a reading to someone I say, "These are the options of how this might play out" but I don't know the level of consciousness of that person, nor do I pretend to tell them they're going live things out in a certain way. These are your options, I say.

Pick an experience where you embody a high vibration or pick an experience where you embody a low vibration, that's on you. That's using your free will. Everything is created at the level of one of the seven planes; I mentioned that before. The vibration in which it is created will bring you results at that same plane.

The sixth chakra is where our gods live. In reality, our "gods" are our parents. The sixth chakra is a void with two lotus petals, one with a sun on the right and with a moon on the left. The void is our throne, where we sit while we own our power, with our parents on either side. The problem is, however, that we don't dethrone our parents. We let them run the show, our entire life, from their low-level consciousness. What thoughts are your perpetrators? What thoughts are continuous? Is your child your god? Is your money your god? Is the size of your penis your god? Is your car your god? Is Spirit your god? What is your god?

Because *that's* the god you're co-creating with. And so, you need to know the level and quality of your thoughts and your consciousness to know what's going to come of those rhythmic cycles that are inherent in your chart; that are inherent in the universe.

No one is trying to make you suffer and have pain but you are limited by the flesh, by the circle, by the cross, by the physical plane. Of course, pain is inevitable. Get over it. No one's going have a holly jolly life, but your level of consciousness is going to dictate how you handle those things and what you learn from them if you choose, or if you believe there's a lesson.

Examining Sticky Note Spirituality Buzzwords Related to the Law of Cause and Effect: "I'm Woke"

Woke refers to the process of waking from a state of sleep. In the levels of consciousness mentioned before, the waking state is called jagrat. The Principle of Cause and Effect is directly related to your sleep or waking state and its relationship to your level of consciousness. If you are unaware of what you are creating, you are still responsible for its effects. However, if you are woke and you're still creating suffering, you're participating in your suffering. Being woke socially refers to social justice issues and political activism, however, the term actually refers to consciousness and the results of what karma you are creating from that state of consciousness.

What's wrong with this notion of woke? People love to say, "I'm so woke." They think it's crystals and yoga mats and Reiki and rattles. In the literature there are four states of being. Woke has to do with identifying the second level, awareness—waking from a dream state. A delusion. It has to do with this idea that you have removed the first veil of illusion. Everything around us is what's called maya or illusion. This does not mean that you're at the Christ consciousness or the Buddha consciousness. You might be aware, you might say, "Oh, everything's a mirror. Oh, my room is messy. I might be a mess. Oh, that person is mean. I'm mean to myself."

Then I'll say maybe you're a little woke—maybe. But are you *really*? Crystals and theories and reincarnation and past lives and chakras and healers? They are not making you woke. Seeing 11:11, the number of awakening, does not make you woke.

If you create karma from a state of sleep, you are unaware of what you're creating. In other words, you're still responsible, but if you're woke, as many say, and you're still holding on to your suffering, your materialism, your aggression, then you are consciously creating that in your life and in the world. If you are so woke as to know about social justice issues and you can't see that you are responsible for having created this world, are you really woke?

Again, "woke" is a higher state of consciousness. This is where age benefits us and this is where astrology benefits us, but you don't need to know astrology to appreciate or understand everything I am trying to convey. You know if you're dating the same guy over and over and over and over again for the past fifty years there's a problem. You keep creating/attracting the same guy from the same level of consciousness. You know that you need to be "woke" and shift your consciousness but this doesn't mean you will. Awareness is not enough!

The Stages of Behavior Change

In public health behavior-change models like the Transtheoretical Model of Behavior Change, the first stage is Precontemplation. Let's call this "the sleep state." You may not even be aware there's an issue. However, once you become aware of it, you enter the Contemplation stage. That doesn't necessarily mean that you initiate change. The third stage is Preparation in which you are still mulling things over and maybe making small steps to change, however, still not that much.

The next stage is Action, where you actually start making changes. This is an actual shift in consciousness that will really change your course of action, your karma. After Action there is Maintenance, which is a daily battle until the change becomes innate. Unfortunately, the model speaks to relapse: when most people return back to precontemplation and ignore the previous woke state. In essence nothing has changed and the Law of Cause and Effect continues on as it always has from the moment of conception; from a low level of consciousness, because belief change did not occur. Transmutation did not occur.

I have a three-pronged model for behavior change called the band-AID. *A* is for awareness, *I* is for Integration, and *D* is for doing-it-differently. Again, awareness is not enough. Multiple studies have confirmed that awareness is not sufficient for behavior change. Knowing the law of karma is not enough for you to stop doing wrong deeds. Integration is the process of beginning to get woke. You are starting to take responsibility for your life and the results of your past actions, whether you can identify them specifically or not, and you are beginning to realize that you do have agency in your life.

This is the space where you start integrating the shadow of your parents and gain consciousness around the opposites in your life, understanding you've been trying to live life on one side of the coin rather than integrating both sides of it.

Integrating the Shadow and Finding the Midpoint

As you integrate your shadow aspects you begin living more fully. When you consciously decide to do things differently in this lifetime—and I am referring to doing things differently from your parents—you are entering higher levels of consciousness and you actually start changing the energetic patterns around the laws of karma. In my podcast "The Mistress of the Subconscious" I discuss different themes that we all struggle with.

Let's explain this by taking an example and unpacking it. Our example will the prostitute-nun complex. Drawing upon our pendulum, we have the prostitute at one far end and the nun at the other. The prostitute is at the 0 point of the pendulum and the nun is at the pendulum point of 100. The midpoint of 48 to 52 is at the center. A female client of mine was having difficulty reconciling two extremes of her personality when it came to sex, and her behavior reflected this. She had had an indiscriminate sexual encounter in a closet as a teenager, not even remembering the person's name or face. As an adult, she lived as an archetypal nun rarely having sex with her husband in an attempt to purify that first sexual encounter. So, in either case she was living at either the 0 or the 100; she was living at the extremes.

We wanted to bring her back to the midpoint range, so I advised her to reconcile these extremes by defining a nun and a prostitute and then defining the midpoint between the two. We have false, limiting beliefs imposed on us by our parents' value systems, our unintegrated shadow, and social and cultural contexts. They are arbitrary and random. We hold ourselves to these extremes without ever defining what they mean to us. Once we demystify them by defining them in terms we can understand, we can live much more freely. This particular client realized her mother had had only one sexual partner: her father. She herself was holding herself to this same standard, but she had already had more than one sexual partner, so she became the nun in her marriage in an attempt to honor her mother's behavior and purify the previous sexual experience she'd had.

We can manipulate the subconscious by integrating these midpoints, the 48 to 52. This is what it means when the law says, "All paradoxes can be reconciled."

When we are at the 0 or 100, we are in the animal state of consciousness. Being at the 48 to 52, the midpoint, means being in a divine state of consciousness. In my book *The Seven Gates* I discuss the discovery of one's divinity through one's humanity. Your attempt to be "god" represents your own attempt to get from the 0 or 100 to the midpoint of 48 to 52, which is where we should all strive to be.

WHO ARE THE CHARACTERS IN *YOUR* LIFE?

In the book *The Seven Gates* I discuss the seven deadly sins or the *ripus* of Hinduism. In my latest workbook *Dethroning Olympus*, I use the language of the enneagram to make sense of the 0 to 100. An embodiment of the deadly sins is represented by 0 and the virtues represent the 100. The humanity of who we are is the midpoint. We need to honor both sides of the coin for we are both virtuous (as revealed by the contents of our good buckets) and deadly (as revealed by the contents of our bad buckets/shadow). I teach clients fairy tales so that they can refer to them to name the characters in their lives. I use 0 as Aladdin (my humility), Jafar as 100 (my pride), and the Genie (my balanced self) is my 48 to 52.

When I choose to show up as a child (0 to 100) I am reverting back to my child script and the origin story I inherited at conception, which as we know, represents the lowest level of consciousness. When I choose a higher level of consciousness, the adult, I am in the 48 to 52 range, and honoring my divine spark.

If you show up as the 0, the members of your family have to show up as the 100, because that's what's left. If you show up as 80 percent in your marriage, your spouse only has to show up for 20 percent. If you show up as 0 (no power) you will overcompensate, as per the principle, in another way. You may have road rage for instance to "show that guy" you have ultimate power.

Remember, we always want to strive to be at the 48 to 52. I am a believer that most people are what I call a "little to the left" or a "little to the right" of the 48 to 52. If you are born in a new moon phase to a full moon waxing phase, you tend to find comfort in the 30 to 45 range, putting you a little to the left of the 48 to 52.

If you are born from the full moon to the balsamic moon, you tend to find comfort in the 60 to 75 range, the waning phases, so you're a little to the right.

In my case I was born in a first quarter moon phase. You can find your moon phase in your astrological chart or by googling the phase that the moon was in the day you were born. In Ayurveda there is a concept called *prakriti*, which represents the state of the body at the moment of birth. There is as well the *manas prakriti*, the state of the mind at the moment of conception. Both of these prakriti states should be balanced if you are to function optimally.

I am a water and air person, therefore, as a subconscious counselor (water and air) I am honoring my manas prakriti and am in balance. Many people ask how to find their purpose. The answer is to honor your elemental balance, your moon phase, and the values you appreciate that are in your buckets, and reduce the judgments around those values. That's the recipe to mastering this principle.

Shifting the Midpoint

Getting back to the 48 to 52 for a moment, Odysseus is the perfect metaphor of someone who left home, returned home, and understood (by integrating and doing things differently) that you need to be a little to the left or right, but you cannot separate the olive branch from the marital bed. The symbolism of the marital bed speaks to your parents' voices living in your subconscious throughout your entire life, and owning the fact that they may be the dominant voices inside your head. They are both a competitive and collaborative voice. However, if you can manipulate your pendulum a little to the right or left and find your own voice by doing things a little bit differently, you can own the value system your parents gave you at conception while reducing the judgments about the contents of their bad buckets and your parents themselves.

You cannot make a radical departure from your parents in that ultimately your behavior can't end up being all that different from their behavior as brought to life by the contents of their good and bad buckets. However, you do need to shift a little and do things differently than they did, so you can assume control of your own life. Find the range between the 0 and the 100 that you are comfortable with, ideally in the neighborhood of the 48 to 52.

THE FOUR STATES OF CONSCIOUSNESS

Now let's discuss states of consciousness with a little more scrutiny. There are four states of consciousness, which, according to Mauricio Puerta (a professional astrologer and my teacher) are represented by 1) rock, 2) water, 3) wine and 4) blood.* When you are totally asleep, you are a rock. If you're not a rock anymore, you've gained some awareness. When you are woke, you're in contemplative awareness. However, just because you've removed the veil and you understand that this is all illusion, and this is all energy, and that you can cite *The Kybalion*—none of that means you're woke. Show me your life. Show me at what level of consciousness you're creating and then you can tell me you're woke. At this phase perhaps you're starting to integrate, but you're still not fully committed. Some things begin to shift, but huge shifts aren't occurring yet, so now you are water.

At this point you've got some intuitive feeling or intuitive vibration going on, but water is also a very low level of consciousness. This has to do with the womb, and the water of the womb is toxic and parisitic. The water element is intuitive and feeling, but it keeps one in a state of being a child, of seeking someone outside oneself to meet one's needs.

The third level of consciousness is wine. Here you are aware of what you are and have a desire to stop being a being of low consciousness. Wine is considered one of the two higher states of consciousness. It's like the air element. It's perceptive, has logic, exhibits rational thought about consequences, but is still limited because it can get stuck in dogma and/or right and wrong. You still can go higher in consciousness.

Higher than wine is blood, as in the blood of Christ. This is the highest form of consciousness. At the levels of wine and blood you're doing things differently, actually changing your life consciously, and shifting energetic karmic patterns from this life and possibly past lives. Blood is correlated with fire. The fire element represents the process of transmutation. Only when you transmute your consciousness can you change your life using the same energy, planet, or archetype. Your objective is to live with the highest conscious expression of those planets, energies, or archetypes—whatever you choose to call them; semantics aren't important. This is life being lived at the highest level of consciousness, a transmutation of what you were to what you have become.

Jesus, at the Marriage at Cana, turned water to wine, which were found in barrels made of rock. At the Last Supper, Jesus poured four cups of wine. The last represented the cup of redemption and signaled the release of the new covenant written in blood. In Matthew 26:28–30 and Luke 22:20 (NIV) Jesus surmised, This wine is my blood, which will be poured out to forgive the sins of many and begin the new agreement from God to his people.

We all aspire to Christ consciousness but don't forget, we come with limitations. I told you about squares and oppositions in your chart. The two planets that are involved have a low-level consciousness and a high-level consciousness, and you get to choose which one you would like to manifest or exhibit. The energy of Mars for instance, which is conflicted at its lowest level—can be raw, it can be anger, it can be fighting, it can be killing. At its high level it can be accommodating, it can be agreement, it can be consolidating, it can be meeting eye to eye, where conflict leads to some agreement, where both parties win.

If we understand the highest level of consciousness of each planet (from four states of consciousness/animals at the four levels) we can choose to live at the highest state of consciousness every time we undergo a planetary cycle.[5] I'm a believer in the 80/20 principle: Live

---

5 Please see page 157 in the appendix for all twelve astrological signs and the four levels associated with each sign.

at the highest (adult) consciousness 80 percent of the time and remain at a lower level of consciousness (child) 20 percent of the time.

Remember, you can't choose the transits in your life, but you can choose how to handle them. Just because the chart indicates something is coming—a limitation, a struggle, a transit—you get to decide how you're going to live it out. But don't think that advocating for "positive vibes only," and being in denial or being delusional represents a high state of consciousness. That's the lowest state of consciousness. That's the rock. So at least be aware. If nothing else, be aware. Feel your feelings.

And if anyone asks, admit that you're having a shitty day.

CHAPTER 8

The Seventh Law— The Principle of Gender

THIS LAW STATES, "Gender is everywhere. Everything has its masculine and feminine principles. Gender manifests on all planes." This law is often explained as the Yin/Yang principle. In the Yin (shadow, cold, feminine principle) there is a dot of black, which represents Yang. In the Yang (action, warm, masculine principle) there is a dot of white, which represents Yin. Males have estrogen and females have testosterone. Both masculine and feminine energies exist in everything.

In astrology, the feminine polarities are the earth and water signs and the masculine polarities are the fire and air signs. Taurus, Virgo, Capricorn are earth; Cancer, Scorpio, Pisces are water; Aries, Leo, Sagittarius, are fire; Gemini, Libra, Aquarius are air.

On the crosses in astrology, we find both feminine signs and masculine signs to balance out each.

In mythology, Aphrodite and Ares were lovers, which represent the masculine and feminine energies in relationship. Independent of gender and sexual preference, masculine and feminine energies exist in every couple. Shiva Shakti is the Hindu representation of the perfect balance of masculine and feminine energies. Dionysus in Greek mythology is twice-born because he balanced his masculine and feminine energies.

What's wrong with this word *soulmate* and how does it apply to the Principle of Gender?

The word *soulmate* has several origins. In the new age tradition, it was popularized by the prophets and meant a person you have spent many lifetimes with and that you have a specific mission this time around to fulfill together. In tarot, it is believed to be an intertwining of souls, particularly sexual in nature, who have a shared fate. In theosophy, an esoteric religious movement, it is believed that God created androgenous souls, half-male and half-female. Upon incarnation, these were split into one gender or the other and they went out seeking a partner, their soulmate. They then meet up with this "missing half" for a specific purpose. Or they unite to burn karmic debt, which, when completed, fuses these souls back together again so that they are whole once more.

I am not a believer in the idea of a soulmate for it implies that there is only one significant other for all of us. And because of my channelings, experiences with clients, and an understanding of the Principle of Vibration, I believe that this term has been radically misused. I like to use the example of a ladder instead. There are souls on the A rung, the B rung, the C rung, and so on and so forth. Each congregates on a specific rung of the ladder that measures their level of spiritual maturity and vibration.

Introducing the Threadmate

Upon incarnation you have a "vibration" and while on Earth you meet up with other souls who have that same vibration. More often than not they become sexual partners, but soulmates are not exclusively sexual partners. In my book *The Truth Is in the Triangle*, I rename the soulmate concept *threadmate*. A threadmate is someone we come to be in relationship with for a specific purpose. (I'm using relationships as an example; however, it can be friendship or business relationships too.) In my book, I explain that we are threaded together by a specific vibration; that is how we meet. However, we in the earthy realm decide the purpose of that relationship and there are rules around how we maximize the relationship to meet karmic objectives.

When you meet someone and decide to engage in relationship, sit down and identify the thread that brought you together. Is it building a family, building a business, having sex? There is no wrong or right answer. Simply identify one thread that you both agree is the thread linking you together. For instance, my partner and I stated that balance and growth were our threads.

Next, each person needs to be clear on one or two non-negotiables. Provide these to the other partner. These are clear boundaries set by each, bookends so to speak, so that everyone can navigate the relationship clearly.

These non-negotiables are clear markers and it should be understood by both parties that if they're violated, it's time to either renegotiate the relationship or leave it. The thread will speak to the unmet needs of each person. No one was loved unconditionally and you were there to meet your parents' needs, not the other way around. When we enter relationships, we have a naïve understanding that the person is supposed to meet our needs. This is a false conception. Nobody is supposed to meet your needs, only you. However, we do have earthly needs and desires, and we do get into relationships for multiple reasons, so meeting needs is somewhat of an expectation. But that said, it's also true that we never get entirely clear on how this should manifest day by day, often resulting in arguments and blowouts; no one signed up to be everything for you.

THREADMATE V SOULMATE

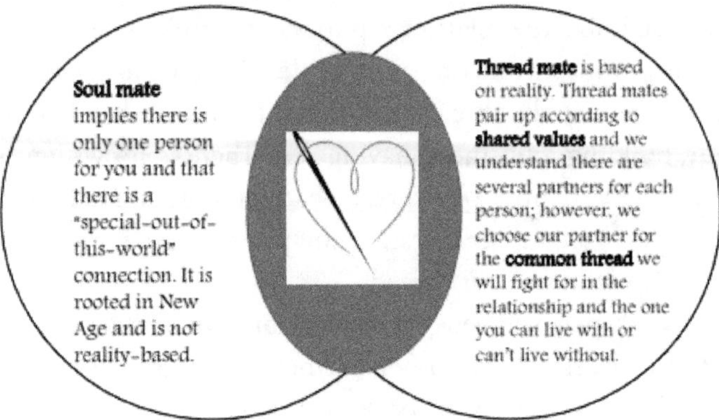

So, let's get clear. The way to experience God is through the feminine principle and the five senses. The five senses, especially sight, have to do with the fire element, which pertains to transmutation. This is the ultimate goal of spirituality: to transmute a lower level of consciousness to a higher level of consciousness. In relationships, we tend to stay in child mode, to exhibit fuzzy thinking, and to blame our partner when things go south. Since your partner will be called to meet at least one of your needs, get clear about what that is. In my relationship, my partner mirrors for me what I need to do and become. That is the need he fulfills, which is linked to our thread of balance and growth.

Sit down with your threadmate again and identify what need he or she will fulfill. Know that fights are inevitable, and also that you and your partner can grow in two different ways when arguments arise. First, ask yourself what is this person mirroring back to me about myself? Next, ask yourself, How does this fight relate back to the unmet need I have that my partner promised to meet? If it does not, it is a need you need to meet for yourself, and is not to be carried under the weight of the relationship.

For instance, say your thread is to build a million-dollar business with your partner. Your need might be to meet your financial needs by having money in the bank so you feel secure financially. However, your partner cheats on you and you decide to divorce. I invite you to go back to the thread and the realize that his or her cheating has nothing to do with the need you have for financial security. You need to turn back to yourself, and realize what this is mirroring in you and not blame your partner. Every five to seven years the system will crack and it is an opportunity to renegotiate a new thread and a new need.

These renegotiations are ruled by Saturn, the planet of karma, and you may realize it's time to end the marriage. It is a karmic influence, but you are employing your free will to make your decision. If you and your partner are still vibrating at the same frequency because you have not transmuted, you will inevitably repeat that same pattern with your next partner. You have a choice, at anytime, to end a relationship, but do not call it karma. The law influences a renegotiation, an opportunity to do it better. However, in this you employ free will and employing it, you can end the relationship if you want something different. If your vibration or that of your partner has shifted, then the likelihood of the two souls remaining together is improbable. Oftentimes people stay together on paper, but the actual relationship is over. This is the same thing.

Identifying Your Preferred Parent

In childhood we created a wrong alliance with one parent, male or female. We created a wrong alliance based on a power currency: overt power or covert power. If you lean more toward loud outbursts, aggression, and anger, that is overt power. Whichever parent displayed that communication style is your preferred parent. It is a wrong alliance and linked to the masculine polarity.

Whichever parent was more covert, perhaps playing the victim and/or was passive-aggressive and manipulative—that is an example of covert power currency and the feminine polarity. We need both; we have both. And we should have both in equal proportions, but we do not. Out we go into the world to meet a partner to complement the other polarity, the one we lack. This has nothing to do with sexuality, gender, or sexual orientation. Masculine and feminine polarities are found in everything in nature, and in everyone.

Your power currency, let's say overt, leans toward the masculine polarity, so you subconsciously seek someone to balance that energy and you attract feminine polarity or covert power currency.

Relationships are mirrors to what we are lacking and the other person simply mirrors the opposite polarity so we can become whole beings within ourself. My partner is patient and consistent; these are feminine polarity traits. I on the other hand am impulsive and inconsistent. He mirrors the qualities that I need in order to balance the feminine polarity and live in balance in accordance with the Principle of Gender. This principle is the highest understanding of universal law we can attain. Human beings cannot comprehend the magnitude of the universe and the ALL is Mind law. We think hierarchically and the ALL is Mind is cyclical; the mind of God is something we cannot envision in our dense Earth state.

The Principle of Gender is the most pervasive of the laws in our psyche because it seeps into our relationships, our personality style, and our sexual orientation. We are born from an egg and a sperm, a masculine and feminine principle, and balancing these energies is at the crux of who we are and what we are here to do. In yoga we speak of a coiled serpent at the base of the spine. This is called kundalini, and when this energy, represented by the serpent, arises and begins its ascent up the spine of the initiate, a spiritual awakening in that individual is bound to occur.

This serpent represents the masculine and feminine polarities in our first chakra, our foundation, our parents. We can only raise kundalini through a transmutation of consciousness. When you finally decide to stop living your parents' unlived lives and live your own, you can begin to raise kundalini. You can do breath work, yoga asanas, and meditate, however, kundalini is only raised with higher consciousness and a balance of your masculine and feminine polarities. In the caduceus, the staff of Hermes Trismegistus, the two coiled serpents represent the Principle of Gender, the masculine and feminine principles.

Uniting Our Energies in the Sixth Chakra

While we struggle with which polarity, currency, or in determining which parent we prefer, we are out of balance. We are only raising one of the serpents, either the right side or the left side. This is duality. Once you accept that you need to integrate the polarity or power currency that you negated earlier in your life, you can raise the opposite serpent, the opposite polarity. Upon reaching the sixth chakra, when they unite, then you can have clear sight.

The sixth chakra resembles a two-flowered lotus. On the right side is the sun, the masculine principle. On the left, the moon, the feminine principle; hence, your mother and father. In the middle of the chakra is what is known as the void, which we mentioned earlier. This is your throne—the space for you to unite your energies and assume your power. Only with the balancing of the masculine and feminine principles will you achieve balance and stability. The sixth chakra is coveted as the seat of consciousness and is linked to the Principle of Gender, however, without a balance of both, you will not be able to raise your consciousness very far.

The snake, serpent, or dragon in myth and story are metaphors for low-level consciousness. The snake slithers and indicates separateness from Self and from God. As we raise the serpent, only through higher vibrational choices and higher consciousness, can we begin to ascend spiritually up the chakras and in our life. The completion of the Principle of Gender is symbolized by the serpent Ouroboros, a snake or dragon swallowing its tail, symbolizing wholeness or infinity.

Again, the circle is representative of the universe, which is incomprehensible to the human mind. Thus, the Principal of Gender, and through the balance of energies, is how humans can achieve true spiritual progress. This motif is repeated in many mythologies, oftentimes represented by a transgender god, representing the unification of the masculine and feminine principles.

Shiva-Shakti, Yin-Yang, and Anima-Animus

The Shiva-Shakti principle is common in Ayurveda and yoga. In Greek mythology, Dionysus, the god of wine and pleasure, is represented with a thyrsus, a staff with a pine cone atop. Dionysus is a transgender god, representing the Principle of Gender. He is considered the god of wine and pleasure because only true balance and stability (pleasure or what some would call happiness) is achievable upon this merging of energies; the pine cone represents the pineal gland.

The pineal gland is responsible for the dark and light regulation of sleep cycles. In a spiritual sense this represents the light and dark of our parents, our light and shadow aspects, and the balance of the two—the masculine and feminine.

The Yin-Yang symbol represents the Principle of Gender and is as well represented by the function of melatonin in the pineal gland; light within the dark, dark within the light. The Yang principle is masculine and the Yin principle is feminine.

Carl Jung wrote extensively about the anima and the animus as part of the collective unconscious. The anima to him was the female principle in the male. The animus was the masculine principle in the female. I view the anima and the animus the way Jung described them: like dots in the Yin-Yang symbol wherein there is a white dot in the black part of the image and a black dot in the white part of the image.

These energies of the anima and the animus are no longer unconscious; they're alive and well and part of our everyday vocabulary and our culture in general. One of the reasons why we're seeing an increase in transgender individuals in our society is because we're reaching a point where people are actually balancing the masculine and the feminine energies within themselves. The transgender is the embodiment of the Law of Correspondence coming to fruition. We're trying to achieve that 48 to 52 internally and it is being articulated externally as part of our cultural expression.

Within the sixth chakra, within the void, is a downward triangle, and the *om* symbol. This represents the feminine polarity at its highest vibration. Downward triangles always represent Earth and water, which is feminine.

Om, which we have mentioned before, is a sacred mantra that encompasses the masculine, feminine, and neutral principles, all of which are needed for any creation. It is important to understand that within the sixth chakra the masculine and feminine principles meet. The three energies necessary for creation are involved and, as just stated, a downward triangle, representing the feminine polarity, is present. The downward triangle means that once you have achieved balance and higher consciousness, you are to return to the first chakra to do it all over again. This time, however, you do so based on a new vibration, a new foundation. This time you need to go to the fourth chakra, which is where the masculine and feminine live in communion with others. You can only go to the fourth chakra when you have a new foundation, when you are living in your power, when you are speaking truthfully, and when your masculine energies are balanced.

In the myth of Hercules in the Garden of Hesperides, Hercules meets Atlas on the path. Hercules has been tasked with getting three golden apples from the garden. At one point he offers to help Atlas carry the weight of the world. When Hercules temporarily carries the world on his shoulders, Atlas enters the garden and grabs the three apples for Hercules.

These three apples refer to Love, Wisdom, and Service. Only when our energies are balanced, when we are living in truth, right mind, and a high vibration, can we enter the fourth chakra of unconditional love to the other and, like Hercules, carry the other's burden. In the myth, Hercules is told, "The *Way* to us is always marked by service. Deeds of love are signposts on the *Way*."

Many people think that by being a martyr or a rescuer they are being of service. You cannot truly be of service until you balance your energies and raise your consciousness. Then and only then can you drop back into the heart center and serve another. Prior to that your behavior can be considered to be selfish. You are taking something from yourself and from the other.

Integrating the Unintegrated Parent

In *The Seven Gates*, I discuss that every person, place, thing, or situation represents the mother or father. We create negative situations in our life in an attempt to get our needs met. Between the ages of zero and seven we did not get our needs met, and every situation, no matter who or what it contained, really represents our parents (symbolically). Usually one of our parents, the one we don't have the similar power currency with or the wrong alliance with, is the symbolic parent who shows up. This is an attempt to balance the masculine and feminine energies in our psyche.

For example, I share an overt power currency with my father, so my mother (the feminine in my case) was unintegrated. I kept marrying my "mother" (symbolically) as an attempt to integrate the feminine. When I realized I could integrate her myself, in my own psyche, I stopped attracting my mother in my partners. I balanced my energies internally.

This is a representation of balancing the internal masculine and feminine energies. When I learned of my breast cancer, I immediately understood that I had castrated the feminine aspect of my life in an attempt to eliminate my mother (feminine polarity) from my psyche. I had preferred my father's very overt power currency and had followed his cues. One of the greatest lessons for me was integrating my mother, my feminine principle, to become whole.

One year after my breast surgery I had a Birth of Venus party for myself and invited all of my female friends. I had a friend sing opera and we danced Celtic goddess dances on a labyrinth and wore beautiful headdresses and flowy dresses. Venus or Aphrodite is the goddess of beauty and love (both erotic and agape love) and represented the female aspect of myself that I had rejected. In an attempt not to integrate my mother, I had neglected my image and anything beautiful. This acknowledgement of the female principle inside me was the beginning of my healing. Once I healed from cancer, five years later, I celebrated with a *Heiros Gamos* ceremony, which I mentioned briefly earlier.

Heiros Gamos is a marriage of oneself to the god of one's choice. It represents the marriage of the feminine and masculine polarities that exist within all of us. I had to come full circle and balance the masculine and feminine energies inside in order to be whole. In my book *The Truth Is in the Triangle*, I discuss the *Heiros Gamos* ceremony and provide a workbook to create a *Heiros Gamos*, or mystical marriage in yourself and with your partner.

The imbalance of these energies within us attracts a partner with the same balance of energies; albeit the opposite. If you are the male archetype in the relationship 70 percent of the time, your partner can only represent the masculine archetype 30 percent of the time. The same goes for the female proportion. I see this as a huge problem in relationships these days, especially in the sexual relationships of couples. *The Truth Is in the Triangle* is a model to work the masculine and feminine energies in the relationship so the system is balanced and everyone is satisfied. It is also my belief that the transgender community is growing because the balance of masculine and feminine energies—starting from the material plane through the cosmos—is out of balance. The emergence of the transgender community is an attempt to balance our psyches and reestablish a balance with the feminine and masculine polarities, the Principle of Gender in action.

Examining Sticky Note Spirituality Buzzwords Related to the Principle of Gender: "Divine Feminine" or "Divine Goddess"

Here is another construct prevalent in our world today. What is meant by the *Divine Feminine* or *Divine Goddess*, and how does it relate to the Principle of Gender? Well, culturally the world is in the midst of a big pendulum flip right now. When paganism ruled the day, many cultures all over the world were matriarchal in nature. Christianity took over and the orientation swung all the way to the left by becoming masculine. We went to the extreme of toxic masculinity, which absolutely needs to be gotten rid of. Now we're swinging back toward the Divine Feminine.

I'm all for paying my bills, and I'm all for calling the shots and all that, don't get me wrong, but you need to have balance within. Women are castrating men now; the way women were castrated before. Neither construct works according to this law. If you're a woman but you're very masculine, the men you attract are castrated, because you're the man. That's one way this manifests. Just like if you're a very feminine man, you might attract very masculine women. And this doesn't matter if you're homosexual, it doesn't matter if you're bisexual—it's just an energy; it has nothing to do with sexuality.

The myth of Dionysus is one of my favorite myths. He's considered a twice-born god. According to the story he was burned to a crisp; the only thing that was saved was his heart. Athena takes his heart and sticks it into Zeus's thigh and he's reborn. The thigh here symbolizes our lower nature or the animal self, and the feminine or the heart represents our higher nature, the Divine. It also represents the fourth chakra versus the second chakra. The Principle of Gender enters into this given that Dionysus is a transgender god, born first of lower consciousness and then of higher consciousness.

Gender Extremes

As I was saying a little earlier, we've swung from one gender extreme to the other over the course of mankind's history. Initially matriarchy was the norm before being replaced by cultures ruled by the patriarchy. If you ever saw *Wonder Woman*, the beginning scene is set on the island of the Amazonians. The Amazonian women were not allowed to have men on the island except to have sex with them. They would kick them off the island and they would castrate their sons if they had male children. It was all about the feminine.

Yes, there was one thousand years of peace but really knowing what we know about the polarities, this has to tell you something about what we came from. The feminine expression was so extreme in those days that the pendulum, when it swung, swung all the way to the other side—to the toxic masculine. If the matriarchal culture had been a bit more balanced, we probably wouldn't have created such a toxic masculine culture.

In school we are taught about the British monarchy. To my way of thinking, Queen Victoria and Queen Elizabeth are what I call bookends: they were both queens with no kings; instead, their husbands were princes. These queens were at the extremes on the 0 to 100 scale. All of the kings/queens that were in the middle of the bookends had partners who conformed to the establishment. Those in the 48 to 52 (the neutralizers of the pendulum) were King Albert who abdicated, Princess Diana who died, and Meagan Markle. They tried to shift the system but failed. If you look at your relationships, you probably show up as a queen with no king. A prince that is castrated (like Prince Charles), the abdicating king who left the system—these are both examples of the Principle of Gender in play.

The Amazonians were strong women who castrated men; women today are against toxic masculinity and castrate men. This represents a shift of the pendulum. The transgender community is the neutralizer. The Amazonians are a wonderful representation of the Principle of Gender, the *Heiros Gamos*, within ourselves. They chopped off their right breast, the masculine principle. As mentioned, they allowed men on their island only for sex and they carried their children on their left hip, the feminine side of the body. In our society the only energy that is valued is the masculine energy, represented by Mars, the warrior archetype.

Gender energy in our modern world has gone awry. The low vibration of Mars is represented by anger, aggression, and violence—the tyrant king. However, the high vibration is an orderly king. I equate it to Saturn. It's masculine, but authoritative, stable, and structured. The feminine polarity at a low vibration is the Venus archetype, *Aphrodite Pandemos*, featuring beauty, makeup, manicured nails, and selfies. However, the high vibration Venus, *Aphrodite Urania*, is represented by mirth, elegance, and laughter, the three Graces in mythology and their counterparts, the nine Muses.

Today we are living in such a low vibrational energy of Mars and Venus energy when we have the potential to transmute and have a structured kingdom ruled by love. Venus rules Taurus and Libra. This does not mean that Taurus is of a low vibration and Libra is of a high vibration. However, there are two types of Venus, and they represent eros love and agape love respectively.

These two types of Venus are called Aphrodite Urania and Aphrodite Pandemos. Aphrodite Urania rules air and fire in the astrological chart and Aphrodite Pandemos rules earth and water. Aphrodite Pandemos is eros love, earthly or possession/sexual love, and Aphrodite Urania is linked to agape love, heavenly love. One rules the second chakra, sex, children, and earth-based materiality, while Libra Venus or agape love rules the fourth chakra, love, wisdom, and service. Libra represents balance. When we balance our masculine and feminine energies, we can finally serve humanity like Jesus and Buddha, through a fourth chakra love, not before.

Balancing Gender Polarities

We have to achieve a balance between the Divine God and the Divine Feminine within ourselves so that society as a whole can change. Ask yourself, Am I too masculine? Too feminine? Are I honoring covert power versus overt power? Am I honoring my alliance with my mother and father?

These are indicators to help with this. Look at your sexual relationships if you're in one. That will tell you. That will tell you a lot about the masculine/feminine. There's no wrong or right in terms of how it manifests in your life. But that's one very clear place that, if you examine it, will help you to get a bearing on where this principle is.

The other thing that's happening with this whole Divine Feminine resurgence is that there can be a lot of shame associated with it. And, as mentioned, there's a lot of castration of males, as if males don't know how to behave anymore. I have a lot of clients who have told me, "I don't even know what it's like to be a man anymore. I don't even know what it means."

It means that we don't let males assume male roles. Women want to assume male roles, which is fine, but balance it with a healthy femininity. Your elemental breakdown (air, fire, water, earth) will indicate if you lean more toward the masculine or the feminine. Honor that, but then add the other elements to balance the polarities. Think of it as an orthotic for your soul.

Years ago, I worked at a massage school and the students observed my gait and told me I walked more on my right side than my left. I had noticed the soles of my shoes were more worn out on the right side. This was no shock for the right side is the masculine side. The students recommended that I wear an insole to balance the gait.

Our soul needs an insert as well. You will tend to attract the polarity of the unintegrated parent, the outcast parent. Our response? We tend to criticize those people rather than incorporate that polarity or missing element into our own life. This is a big thing that's happening and again, we're seeing it with the mushrooming of the transgender population. Shiva-Shakti represents the perfect balance of the male/female.

The Shiva Shakti principle is represented here as the divine union between the masculine and feminine principles in Hindu mythology. This image represents the left side, which is the feminine side and the right side, which is the masculine side.

CHAPTER 9

The Eighth Law— The Principle of the Law of Octaves

THE PRINCIPLE OF THE LAW OF OCTAVES includes a lot of the principles we have already explained. This law is not in the actual text of *The Kybalion*; however, it is a metaphysical law. It is also known as the Law of Three, the Law of Seven and the Law of Ninefoldness, and is linked with the enneagram. Gurdjieff, the Armenian philosopher, was not the originator of the enneagram but he did popularize it with his Fourth Way philosophy. He is credited with bringing it back to life and providing an instruction manual as to how it works. The enneagram, and the Law of Octaves associated with it, is believed to have had its origins in theosophy, yoga, hermeticism, and other mystery schools.

Gurdjieff's Fourth Way philosophy is about doing the inner work in your everyday life, not in a monastery, or a cave, or an ashram. The Law of Octaves, also known as the Law of Seven, is the crux of his philosophy. The Law of Seven is also linked to the seven planes in the universe, the number of planets, the days of the week, and mainly the musical scale. The musical scale has seven notes *Do-Re-Mi-Fa-Sol-La-Ti* and the new octave (new level of vibration and consciousness) comes with the next octave of *Do*.

This law describes points that Gurdjieff calls "shocks." These are opportunities to either make a change or return back to your original state of consciousness or inactivity. The first shock comes after *Do-Re-Mi*, between *Mi-Fa*. This is important because the number three is related, as mentioned previously, to thought. You can have a thought around change and the three forces necessary to change (positive, negative, and neutral) and yet not move into the *Fa* (which begins putting things into place at the earthly realm). If you have the thought but don't move into the *Fa*, you will undoubtedly return back to your original state. Nothing will change. The thought is energy so it may materialize as an unhealthy emotion, a physical symptom, or karmic garbage in the world. Energy cannot be created or destroyed, so if a thought is birthed and not followed through on to raise consciousness, it materializes in your body or your life. This relates to awareness and contemplation: without action there is no change.

THE DO-RE-MI AND THE LAW OF THREE

The *Do-Re-Mi* reflects the law of three. It has three syllables, which are represented by a triangle. Remember the Shri Yantra? The triangle represents thought. But again, thought is not enough! Thought is the air element; we need the earth element to bring it to fruition. As we said earlier in this book, the early Christians understood this Law of Three and incorporated it into the expression of the Father, Son, and Holy Ghost. Hinduism features Vishnu, Shiva, and Brahma: a creator, a destroyer, and a balancer. Every religion in every tradition has a version of the Trinity or the Trimurti.

In metaphysics we use the Law of Three. It's the first step in the Law of Octaves or the Law of Sevens or the Law of Ninefoldness. This is the action potential. This is the initiation energy, like I said, and a conjunction brings it into being. There are tons of ideas floating around when I do a reading of the Akashic Records for someone—I see them all the time. But if my client doesn't bring them down and materialize them, nothing happens. You (the client) remain at the Law of Three. That is not enough. You must *begin* a change, and this has to do with the principle of transmutation.

If you know chemistry, this is represented by the triangle, the symbol of delta, which is change. Fire is the only element that can transmute. If you know the story of the Hydra in Greek mythology, it's about Hercules being told, "Do not chop off the head of the Hydra. Two will grow back in its place." The only thing he could do was take a club, set it on fire, and sever the heads of the Hydra because in so doing he was utilizing the element of fire, which is action, doing, transmutation. Again, you can't just *be*. You have to do. That is what actually creates a change. That's the beginning.

Shocking the System

The first point of "shock" (to use Gurdjieff's word, which is a word I use too) follows the note *Mi*, the teenager, or the pause, even the chaos. Here is where we test the waters to see if we can change and if our family, spouse, bank account (for instance) support us in making this change. At the age of fourteen to sixteen teenagers go through this. They test the system to see what the parents will support, what boundaries can be pushed. They are actually trying to live by their own values, and "leave home" in their psyche; this is usually shut down by the parents. The adolescent storm is an attempt to integrate the parents' shadow.

When you are a child, you identify that you have a shadow and you have bad buckets. When you reach the teenage years, you consciously decide to integrate them. You start the process of self-love and forgiveness here, but you do not fully dethrone your parents until you reach *Do*, higher consciousness. You do not own behavior change here yet. This is not higher level of consciousness yet.

This is the point where you stop and consciously decide to actually do something differently in order to make a change. If you do enter the next steps of the Law of Octaves, which are *Fa-Sol-La-Ti*. They represent the number four, which is the number of limitation and boundaries. This is the earth element. This is where we set deadlines and build and construct something in the material world. This step is the action phase.

This shock is the adult, represented by a square. How do you move from child to adult? You move from child to adult by having a plan. This adult phase is a square and it's represented by the number four. In Asian cultures, the number four represents death. Four is death, because it is the earth element and everything on the Earth eventually dies. You cannot be the adult until you actually commit to doing things differently than you have in the past. In *The Seven Gates, The Truth is in the Triangle, and Dethroning Olympus* workbooks I provide an opportunity for readers to define, in measurable terms, their values, needs, and non-negotiables; their philosophy of life. We expect this level of clarity in our employee manuals, but we will not do this with our psyche, our relationships, or our families. If we did, we would be adults and realize how often we betray ourselves. Instead, we choose to not define these things and play the victim rather than stepping into the adult.

Moving Up the Octaves

The *Do* is the next vibration, the next octave up. You need something negative, positive, and neutral to initiate (Law of Three, the triangle, the thought to change), but you have to bring the intention or the thought or the idea to the physical plane (the number four, the element of Earth, structure, discipline, consistency, accountability, the adult). That's what I said before about the square. The square is the number of the Earth, of death, of limitations and of boundaries.

This is where transmutation starts. You start to own the change. This higher level of consciousness starts to be yours. The behavior starts to become second nature. This is where we give an offering or a sacrifice. To enter new consciousness there has to be a death of some sort. This is often a very severe grief process. Again, commitment is adult and change can really only ever happen with a commitment. The only way to start integrating your parents is to commit to your behavior change, which when transmuted, becomes belief change.

Earth is the only element that represents death. That's why it's represented by the ground. That's why it's represented by nature. That's why it's represented by rock, which is a very dense energy. Water, as we have established, is one step less dense, but we don't create with water, we create with earth. With earth we bring that idea that you had into practice, but how exactly do you do this?

You write a rule book, you get a calendar, you set a deadline, you pay money to start a business, you build an empire. The earth element is the only thing that will actually see you through when you want to create change. For people like me who wanted to live without the earth element and have no earth in their chart, it's hard.

Now, even though you're on your path to creating, you can't create because you're eliminating the most important part of the law, which is *Fa-Sol-La-Ti*. Only when you finish the octave fully; when you have the thought; when you set it into motion; when you put it into place with money, with boundaries, with structure, with rules, with management—whatever that is, that Earth element—can you raise to the next vibration, which is *Do*.

Getting to "Do"

This is consciousness raising, and it follows the same law. You have the thought around it. You think, "I'm going to change, but now I have to put my idea into practice to make that change." Every single New Year's Eve resolution ever made got stuck at the shock of *Mi*, and never went to *Fa-Sol-La-Ti-Do*. It's that simple. *You need the earth element.*

Do is higher consciousness. This is you at a higher vibration. This is the only way to raise vibration. This is a different level of consciousness than what you inherited from your parents at conception. This is a circle. In the last *Do* you actually dethrone them and do things differently. This is where you actually burn karma. This is considered transmutation.

The circle is Spirit, the circle is wholeness, the circle means it's yours. Now you own this, in your psyche, in your soul, and in your next lifetime. You don't have to learn this lesson again.

This is all about consciousness. To raise your level of consciousness, you first have to decide that you're going to live at a different level of consciousness. That's the Law of Three. And now put it into place by not fighting, biting your nails, eating the cookies—whatever your thing is. This is the only way to shift the vibration. The Law of Vibration speaks about what vibration is. The Law of Octaves is the answer. It is the only law that explains how to shift consciousness; the only law that speaks to why behavior change is so difficult.

In *The Seven Gates* I discuss the child, the teenager, and the adult. This model is based on the Law of Octaves. This law is based on the musical scale. Venus is the connection with God and Self, in the here and now, on Earth. Venus is the tool of the gods, to tame the beast (ego) within. God is not an afterlife; God is not later. God is here, now, through love, compassion friendship, music, dance, the Graces and the Muses, and so on and so forth now and into eternity.

The entire universe is a circle. Within the circle, there are triangles (thoughts) and squares (physical). The universe is cyclical—spherical and not hierarchical. There are no straight lines in nature, because the universe is a circle, and we are all one within that circle—we are all equal.

DO RE MI (shock)   FA SOL LA TI (shock)   DO

Child	*Teenager*	*Adult*	*Transformation to Transmutation*	*New Vibration*

Triangle Thought Mental Plane 3 Child Awareness Same level of consciousness as parents at conception	Square Earth Physical Plane 4 Adult Integration Different level of consciousness as parents at conception Accountability Define and measure what you want Transformation: Change is still not yours, you still think before you act and you consciously decide to stay in adult	Circle Ether Akashic Plane 7 Do it differently Dethrone your parents TRANSMUTATION: Change is yours. It has become part of your vibration and you now vibrate at this new level. Your karma has changed.

CHAPTER 10

Cultivating a Spiritual Practice

WE HAVE TO CULTIVATE A SPIRITUAL PRACTICE. How do we do this? Find a tradition that speaks to you. Do you want to be Jewish? Do you want to be Christian? Do you want to be a metaphysician? Do you want to be an astrologer? Do you want to be an alchemist? It's all the same. If you strip down various traditions the world over, the practice and the teachings are the same; discernment, right mind, right action—truth.

FINDING A PHILOSOPHY OF LIFE

The key thing here is to pick a philosophy of life and understand the truths you are subscribing to! Most people don't know what they believe. When I ask them what their philosophy is, they look at me blankly. I once opened the Akashic Records for a client and in her fifth chakra was an empty billboard. She wanted to be a meditation teacher and was complaining that no one was signing up for her classes. When I asked her about her philosophy and methods, she said she didn't know.

How are you supposed to teach meditation without a tradition or a philosophy? Again, the subconscious is responsible for your beliefs that were given to you at conception. If you do not have a philosophy of life that you're choosing you will be loyal to what was given to you, whether you know it or not. So, pick a tradition and study its philosophy. You do not have to buy into everything but discern what you will believe in and subscribe to it.

When I went through my severe depression, I abandoned my spiritual philosophy in an attempt to reconfigure what I believed. When I returned from the dead I believed in the same philosophy, but I fine-tuned it as to exactly how I was going to practice it and questioned some of the traditions I had subscribed to. I now have a clear path for my spiritual life; a map of sorts. Your philosophy of life will be your map to navigate the situations in your life. Gaining an understanding of the metaphysical laws, which you have done in this book, is the first step in determining what your philosophy of life will be.

So, pick one practice and keep with that tradition.[6] If you know one well, all the others should make sense to you too. Start with one backbone and then build. At the end of the day, it's about you. Call it the third chakra. Call it turning inward. Call it self-study. Call it jnana yoga. Call it "man know thyself." If you don't know your own mind, if you don't know what's driving your subconscious thoughts, if you're not honest, if you're living in denial, if you're living in a delusional state, if you don't know that you create it all, if you don't know your state of consciousness, who are you healing?

"Man know thyself, and you will know the wonders of the universe." The reason this is true is because you are a microcosm of all of the seven planes that we've discussed in this book. It's such a fascinating thing to study yourself. And the funny thing is, we are oh so egocentric. My best friend is a chef and I'm an astrologer. We are always invited to parties because, as she says, we have "party tricks." She's the food (earth and fire element) and I'm the astrology (water and air element). People love to be fed and told about their life!

Create a Sacred Space for Your Practice

We've established that *Om*-ing and meditating and using incense and

---

6 Please see page 182 in the appendix for more on the twelve truths of a spiritual practices.

crystals does not, in and of itself, constitute a spiritual practice. These elements can, however, be part of having a spiritual practice. We do want to create sacred space. We are the only culture that has a room for sleeping and sex, we have a room for food for eating, we have a room for our computer, for making money. We are the only culture that does not have any space in our house for our spirit, for our divine spark, for god of our choosing. Look at the size of your house and how much space is dedicated to your spirit. And you're wondering why you're living in scarcity when it comes to your spiritual life.

So how do we create this sacred space?

Most people who are looking to develop their spiritual life have an altar or a desk on which they put a picture of Jesus or Buddha or their equivalent. In Hinduism, the sixth chakra is designated as the *ishvadevatar*, the god with form. Pick the god of your choice and incorporate a visual representation of that god into your practice. A small Buddha statue will do. If you like Ganesha or Krishna, start there. Maybe you have a Native American spirit guide. If so, place a statue or picture of him or her on your desk or on a small table. Having a physical representation of what you're connecting to is important. It serves as a mandala for meditation and concentration.

If you do not resonate with a god or a character in any philosophy, perhaps a Sri Yantra, a mandala, or an image of the chakras is better for you. Using psychometry, hold the relic or statue in your hands and see if it speaks to you. What do you see? How do you feel? If it feels right, bring it home and place it on your altar. You may be more inclined to want some semblance of nature in your sacred space, so maybe use a feather, a stone, or a stick as your totem. If you're unsure which tradition you should choose, begin with the representations of Spirit as statues, rocks, sticks, or cards, then work backward to the philosophy. The relics may speak to you first.

I also recommend the use of a desk, bureau, or closet—somewhere you can house your relics and important spiritual knickknacks.

Develop Intuition

A key component of becoming more spiritual is to develop one's intuition.

A lot of people ask me about intuition. Honestly, it's really not that hard to do, once you know how. Intuition is different from spirituality. Every single human being has intuition even though it may not be very well developed. The truth remains that every single one of us has the little hairs on the back of our neck lift up when we feel something is off. Everybody has a gut instinct. Somewhere, somehow, you've had a voice scream at you, "Stop!" so you don't get into an accident or you're not in the wrong place at the wrong time. Intuition is not reserved for "spiritual people." The idea that it might be is absolute nonsense! However, intuition is only as good as the quality of your thoughts. If you do not obsessively understand your thoughts and where they come from, your intuition will be of poor quality.

Years ago, I was at a spiritual store where a psychic reader would "read" clients and give them spiritual guidance. This "reader" was waiting for a client to show up and she got a phone call. The call turned into a fight and she went outside to field it. She was yelling, screaming, and cursing and apparently had little to no control over her emotions and her thoughts. There was no consciousness around her participation in the conflict—a total lack of self-awareness.

Her client walked in and she took her to the back to conduct the reading. And I wondered, What quality of intuition could a reader without self-awareness or analysis of her own thoughts provide? In my opinion, her low-level consciousness would provide poor intuitive guidance. Everyone has intuition and the ability to develop their claires; however, being an intuitive or a psychic does not equate with being spiritual or having an elevated consciousness. Your intuition is only as good as the depth of your own inner work, and your awareness of your judgements, values, truths, and the removal of your veils.

In certain traditions the elders of the church communicate with various souls who have crossed over and receive guidance from them. Yes, if you're out of a body, you can provide guidance, but again, what level of guidance are you receiving? Think about the reader you're visiting and what their life looks like. Who is providing the guidance?

If you are the reader, how is the message you're giving related to what you need to apply to your own life? What quality of guidance can you provide on the issue if you're not heeding your own advice? The Hercules myth of the Capture of the Doe speaks to raising our vibration from instinct to intellect and then intuition. Are you in control of your emotions, and if so, to what degree? Do you question where they come from and why you're still responding as a child? If you do not know what your thoughts are you won't be able to differentiate between your thoughts and your intuition.

The Six Claires

A way we receive intuitive information is through what's called "the claires." If you sense something through your intuition, through the claires, you need to apply it! If you hear something, it's for you. If you see something, it's for you. If you say something, it's for you. This work is all about you because you have to grow and embody the highest consciousness, the highest potential that you can. There is no "other" in spirituality.

There are six claires: clairvoyance, which is clear seeing; clairsentience, which is clear feeling (where you might get shivers and feel a sensation at the back of your neck or your arms or your legs); clairaudience, where one hears something clearly; clairalience, when one's sense of smell is affected; clairgustance, which affects one's sense of taste; and claircognizant, which is clear knowing. Every single person has all six no matter how developed they are.

Finding a Suitable Teacher

I don't like the word *guru* because I grew up in a cult, but I do respect the word *teacher*. One of the specific gifts of a teacher or a guru is silence. The reason silence is a gift from a teacher or a spiritual mentor—a wise person—is because that individual is emanating a certain heightened vibration and they are teaching the disciple through that emanation. Nothing has to be said.

You're being gifted by just being in the presence of that guru in silence. One of my favorite myths is the myth of Hercules and the Garden of Hesperides. The great theosophical writer Alice Bailey specified that, according to the myth, there are two types of teachers. Busiris will promise you the moon and the stars but he will rob you, which is what the cult leader did to me and what many spiritual con artists do these days by *not* teaching you these laws and taking your power. Nereus, on the other hand, will just nudge you in the right direction so you can continue on your path. Then people who come to you for healing are the beneficiaries of your teachings through your *lived* self, the application of your teachings. So, pick a tradition and find your language; what resonates with you. If it's astrology, if it's alchemy, if it's Christianity, if it's crystals, whatever it is; but do it and do it right.

In the shamanic tradition, the spiritual aspirants often partake in a vision quest. A few days with no food or water in the wilderness is supposed to give you great clarity and identify your purpose. When the vision quest is over and you return to the mainland you are mandated to remain silent. However, those around you will sense in you what messages about your purpose you have received. In the old days your role in the tribe was determined by the vibration you returned with after the quest.

When you do your inner work, your vibration will change. If you transmute the low-level consciousness that you are born with, new people at the same vibration will enter your space and your vibrational shift will be palpable to everyone.

The Importance of Reverence

I am a believer in reverence. A spiritual practice needs reverence. I don't care if it's five minutes but give it five minutes. I read my Akashic prayer every day. I know it by heart but the rules say not to read it from memory, so that's my practice, my reverence, which resembles the reverence of my divine spark.

It's a practice. That's the element of the four in action, of the law of octaves, of the *Fa-Sol-La-Ti-*. The point is to get to the next *Do*, the next octave, the next vibration. The practice is the day in and the day out of doing something mundane and tedious. If it's just lighting incense, if it's just opening sacred space, if it's just saying thank you—do it all the time. Have reverence for your practice and make a space for your practice. Dedicate time to it. When I open sacred space, I do so to eliminate doubt, shame, fear, and guilt.

Doubt is the biggest block to having a union with our divine spark. Most students ask me how I do it and the answer is that I just honor everything. In my life I view everything as guidance because I apply the Law of Correspondence all the time. If I say something and I'm wrong, I'm okay with that because I know I will be wrong at times. I'm not God. However, most times, because I apply the law, I am right and it's because I don't doubt my intuition or guidance.

One day I was talking to a friend about an issue we were having in our friendship. He was watching a horserace at that same moment and when I glanced over at the names of the horses, I immediately understood the answer the universe was providing through the horserace. "The horse named 'A Little Bit of Both' will win," I adamantly stated, and that horse did indeed win. According to the Law of Correspondence, I knew that the conversation we were having needed an answer. The answer to the problem we were discussing was clear: we both needed to yield to the other. The horse's name confirmed that.

This is me using sacred space, eliminating doubt, honoring the universal laws, and responding to the Law of Correspondence. If we learn to live symbolically and with faith that the universe will show us the way, we can live in sacred space all the time. Jung called this being connected to the objective psyche. The renowned philosopher and theologian Henry Corbin termed it the *Mundis Imaginalis* and, as established earlier, Carlos Castaneda called it a Shamanic State of Consciousness (SSC), which varies from the Ordinary States of Consciousness (OSC) that most people live in.

If we understand the Principle of Polarity, we understand we can live in both the OSC and the SSC, which is where I spend most of my time. The ordinary state of consciousness of the Earth (i.e., Virgo/ Jesus the man) and the SSC, the shamanic state of consciousness of the spirit world (i.e., Pisces/Jesus the Christ consciousness), is the balance.

I have also come to understand that problems need both hard edges and soft corners. The hard edges are the SSC and the soft corners are the OSC. When I tackle my problems, I offer myself soft edges. I will pout and cry or stay in child mode 20 percent of the time. I stay attached to the script that reads: "So and so did this to me." However, 80 percent of the time I show up with hard edges, the SSC. I break down the veils of delusion, get honest with myself, and understand I created the situation and that something is being mirrored back to me that I need to address. This is the adult, where I meet my own needs and have agency in my life to transmute the low vibration to a higher state.

Removing the Veils of Delusion

The Dance of the Seven Veils is a dramatic dance performance that was given by Salome for Herod II. It's often depicted as a striptease but it's actually a metaphor for the spiritual process of transmutation. The ancient Sumerians have their own version of this infamous dance. Inanna, a Sumerian goddess of the Upperworld, was invited by her sister Ereshkigal, goddess of the Underworld, to visit her after her husband died. When Inanna began her descent into the Underworld, she had to go through seven doors. At each door an article of her clothing was removed. By the time she arrived at the Underworld she was naked. This metaphor represents the unveiling or transmutation process.

As we really get to know ourselves, we remove the veils of delusion and we get closer and closer to our true Self. This striptease is insinuated in the worldly telling of the story. The dance is a spiritual, alchemical process. As we turn ourselves from lead into gold, we become lighter, we burn karma, and we live in a more balanced and stable state.

In mythology many times prostitutes or seductresses, like Mary Magdalene in the New Testament, Eve in the Old Testament, or Lilith in the Talmud are villainized and deemed to be demonic. These stories are used to instill fear. Quite conversely, these female figures from mythology are the holders of the hidden truths in our psyche and in the universe itself. Lilith, like Hermes Trismegistus, holds the wisdom of the universe.

Lilith was considered to be the first wife of Adam. She refused to be dominated by him, however, and she was sent into exile. She was demonized as an evil killer of children, lethal to pregnant women, and a seductress who was going to seduce your husband away from you. She is often featured with serpent imagery as well as wings, long hair, and demons. This image has been intentionally created to create fear and leave you in the dark.

Traditional religions depict this archetype as demonic to keep you veiled and dependent on religious and spiritual leaders who don't want you to liberate yourself. These teachers know the truth. However, if they keep the teachings hidden, they can control the masses. The Dance of the Seven Veils, the myth of Inanna visiting the Underworld, Persephone's rape by Hades, and countless other stories invite you to not be scared of the wilderness within, but rather get naked with the truth and explore who you really are.

The Underworld is simply a metaphor for the shadow or the bad buckets. Enter the cave and discover the wonders it holds. You cannot embark on a true spiritual journey unless you're willing to enter the darkness. Transmutation is the spiritual process and it requires intense self-analysis, honesty, observation of the low-vibrational thoughts in your subconscious, and using everything and everyone you encounter as a mirror designed to aid you on your spiritual journey.

There are no shortcuts to this process. However, you are guided from the very first crisis you experience to the remainder of your life if you're aware of the universe's cycles and what to look for. You were not thrown in this world without a map and a compass. That said, the great spiritual teachings and information about how to apply them has been kept hidden and only available to the privileged few. The new age and the age of Aquarius is a wonderful time to be alive in that we now have access to these teachings, however, many of them are becoming watered down and taught as "fluff." (As if burning karma, changing your life, and creating a balanced, stable life that you do not want to run away from is easy!)

WATCH OUT FOR FALSE PROPHETS!

Don't become enamored of false prophets. In 2012 the planet Neptune, which rules spirituality and false prophets, entered the sign of Pisces, which is a spiritual sign as well as a sign of false prophets. This is a deadly combination at a low vibration, which is where most of us reside. Many spiritual teachers who are not walking their walk or are preaching fluff, what I call "Sticky Note Spirituality," have emerged and will continue to emerge during this transit. In 2025, Neptune will enter Aries and we will have a domino effect wherein these false prophets will all topple over.

Those who have created dependency among their followers or those who have failed to truly change and have been preaching without substance will be exposed. What concerns me about this is that a lot of children are being born during these years whose families are adherents to these frauds. Those children will have, because of the moment of conception, an incongruence of beliefs and will suffer existential crises as they get older and realize the truth of these false spiritual foundations that have negatively influenced their parents and therefore themselves. Another concern is that many people have fled Western religion in search of Eastern traditions (and rightfully so, given that the views of the church have become so limited).

We as Westerners have an inherently different viewpoint of God and different symbology in our collective unconscious. You don't just leave a Western philosophy in search of an Eastern one without a foundational knowledge of both. Doing so creates a severe fissure in the psyche. Many adults are suffering already because of this incongruence. The next generation, the children of those adults born during Neptune in Pisces, will be the next generation of psychiatric patients if we don't get clear that both philosophies essentially say the same thing.

Nothing in religion or spirituality is truth at the surface—it's dogma and manipulation. Neptune rules the oceans and spirituality, so you must dive deeply into the waters of the subconscious and to deep, hidden pearls of wisdom to really encounter true spirituality.

My purpose in life is to spread truth. Not my truth or your truth, THE Truth—the truth that is found in every religion, philosophy, and tradition since the beginning of time. I was duped by a false prophet, enough for all of us! Again, please refrain from being enamored of spiritual practices that promise easy transformation with crystal bowls, sage, and pendulums. These are fun tools to start a discussion about the universal laws, however, they are accoutrements to your practice, not the practice itself.

Why does this help? Because you are going to have a Negredo. You are going to have a Saturn transit. You are going have a dark night of the soul. And the only thing you can do to get through it is to create sacred space. I think it was the great philosopher and Holocaust survivor Viktor Frankl who said that between the action and the reaction there's a space or a pause. In yogic literature, the space between the inhale and the exhale is where God lives. That's the concept of my model. Between the child and the adult, God lives. God lives in that space where you choose to be the adult and not go back to a replay of the subconscious behaviors of your child self.

When you're depressed or you're sad or your husband left you or your hair fell out or you lost everything in your life, you may be in pain but you don't have to suffer if you have a practice. Not that it's going to necessarily make you feel better, not that it's going to bring anything back, but it is going to help you create a space, a pause, that will remind you that this too shall pass and that life can, and will, be good once more.

Epilogue

THE POINT OF THIS BOOK has been to encourage you to establish a spiritual practice that will help you navigate your life and to more easily weather its challenges. This practice may be built around any one of the eight spiritual laws that this book articulates. They are to be used as tools for you as you establish a spiritual practice and then as touchstones as you advance spiritually.

You have potential, but it's limited. You're bound by Earth, a body, a circle and a cross. Typically, as you go through life, you will be presented with the same problem, just different iterations of it. The good news is that your potential to reach the highest consciousness of the themes you came to work through is unlimited. The universe provides cycles throughout life for everyone to use in order to maximize their spiritual growth. You choose how much you want to grow.

Specifically, every seven years, you're going to go through a spiritual experience (a skinny cow). You can call it a difficult time. You can call it Capricorn, you can call it being existentially lonely, you can call it a death. Or you can call it an invitation, a Negredo. Every tradition has a word for it. Those cycles are intended for growth, to just be. That's why you need the pause. That's why you have the spiritual practice for those moments, so that you can raise your consciousness. Squares and oppositions in the chart are for a lifetime. I love people who tell me, "Oh, I've already worked that out." Please. You're working and working and working because it takes a very long time to turn lead to gold. That's the process of alchemy.

You can have a thought or an idea but if you don't bring the Earth principle into it, the number four, the Law of Octaves, the *Fa-Sol-La-Ti-*, it's not going to manifest. Everything is manifested from the subconscious; that's the bottom line. And it has a level of vibration determined by that wound, that false belief, and that limitation, and it will manifest everywhere. And usually, an individual will operate at one extreme or the other until self-mastery is achieved.

Self-mastery, equanimity, higher consciousness—that's the only spiritual path there is. Again, that's the only thing that any of us are here to do. It's called transmutation and just as manifestation requires the element of earth, transmutation requires the element of fire. *The Kybalion* states, "All are on the path. All progress is a returning home. All is upward and onward."

You already are Spirit by nature and as such you already have the divine spark. However, if you want to reach a higher level of consciousness you have to start with some knowledge, with some teachings, so that you understand everything that's happening to you and you can maximize it.

You can pick one of these laws and build an entire spiritual life and practice around it. Perhaps find the one that you were taught at home. I have a friend whose father used to say "Never let the gas tank get to empty." This is the 0 to 100 principle in action; it's the Law of Polarity. She lives her life based on this law. In the same way you can develop a spiritual practice and base your life on the law of your choosing.

Wisdom is passed down from generation to generation. This wisdom is in your psyche. There's no need to rewrite the story or reinvent the wheel. Pick one of the laws and hold yourself to it. It will change your life and you will be a spiritual aspirant on the path to wholeness.

Onward and upward we go!

Appendix:
The Spiritual Practices Workbook

THE TWELVE SIGNS OF THE ZODIAC AND THE FOUR LEVELS OF CONSCIOUSNESS

Sign	Rock (Lowest level of consciousness)	Water	Wine	Blood (Highest level of consciousness)
Aries	Wolf in sheep's clothing	Sheep	Sacrificial lamb	Golden Fleece: A sign of authority and kingship
Taurus	Golden Calf (mythological)	Bull	Minotaur (mythological)	Bullfighter
Gemini	Gorilla	Chimpanzee	Orangutans	Man and Women
Cancer	Slug	Snail	Hermit crab	Scarab
Leo	Stray cat	Lion	Circus lion	Ringleader
Virgo	Sewer rat	Ant	Bee	Hummingbird
Libra	Earthworm	Caterpillar	Chrysalis	Butterfly
Scorpio	Scorpio	Serpent	Phoenix (mythological)	Eagle
Sagittarius	Donkey	Horse	Centaur	Pegasus (mythological)

Capricorn	Crocodile	Goat with a fish tail (mythological)	Goat	Unicorn (mythological)
Aquarius	Men and women that are asleep	Men and women who are awake	Men and women who are self-ware	Men and women who have transmuted their consciousness
Pisces	Piranha	Fish	Mermaid	Fisherman

We credit Mauricio Puerta with the information contained in this chart, which we have modified from the original.

Cultivating a Spiritual Practice

Workbook & Worksheets

The Twelve Truths of a Spiritual Practice

Everything is a system. Every spiritual tradition is a system. It has steps and takes time, to be accurate a lifetime, to work through all the steps, and often we must repeat the same steps over and over again. The steps below are linked to mythology and happen to correlate to the astrological wheel. However, knowledge of myth or astrology is not needed to work them. These steps are found in every tradition.

My twelve truths are linked to Alice Bailey's book, *The Labors of Hercules*. These myths follow Hercules and the twelve tasks he was given by Hera which were deemed impossible. Hera wanted Hercules dead as she feared he would become immortal. These herculean tasks represent the steps on our spiritual path. The first step is the most important and you will revisit this every day until your last breath. It correlates to the principle ALL is Mind. Just as our thoughts never cease, we never cease needing to observe them. In the myth of *Hercules and the Man-Eating Mares of Diomedes*, Hercules had to gather the mares at least twice to be successful. The mares killed his friend Abderis and he was forced to gather them again. The mares represent our thoughts, which trample us moment-by-moment until we learn to have control over them. This represents looking at our thoughts daily and when we fail, returning back to the drawing board. We must constantly observe our personality and the masks we wear. They keep us in child mode, looking to get our needs met from others rather than meeting our needs for ourselves. We never finish this labor during our lifetime.

In the myth of the *Lernaean Hydra*, Hercules has to defeat his personality and become individuated; live in wholeness as ourselves, integrating both our shadow parts and conscious parts. This step involves loving ourselves despite our imperfections and our low-level consciousness. The individuation process is one of the hardest steps on a spiritual path. It requires deep introspection and stripping away of the masks that we wear to fit in. It is the step where we allow our soul to shine through and direct our purpose. The personality is necessary, but the soul is the director of the show. In Truth Six, Hercules makes another mistake, he kills Hippolyte accidentally for failure to pay attention. Truth Six is linked to purification and how we care for our bodies. In Ayurveda, the three pillars of health are sleep, food and truth. We must eat well and exercise to keep the vehicle of the soul cleansed and purified. Like Hercules, we fail each day and get another attempt at it daily. This is the second labor we will revisit daily. First our thoughts, then the care of our bodies. Our thoughts require spiritual sustenance daily through observation of what we allow to enter our headspace as our bodies require sustenance daily through good food and replenishing sleep; together, these allow us to live in truth.

All traditions at their core are linked to the eight spiritual laws discussed in the book. Strip away the dogma and the characters and you will find them there. If not, the tradition is a false teaching. Every spiritual system says the exact same thing. What is often misrepresented is that you can skip steps or lack of clarity about these steps.

I have listed the myths in order of the practice. Again, you don't need to know myth or astrology to follow these practices. I have also provided some practical tools I've written about in my books and workbooks, in my podcast, and on my YouTube channel so you can incorporate the steps easily into your life. The worksheets contained in this appendix will help you with the twelve truths.

I like to layer other traditions with this one, but I use this one as my base, to make sure I'm addressing all of the truths. If you already have a practice that fits into the truths, add them below. You can build your own practice, mixing and matching, but don't skip any truths. Last, remember that your spiritual growth began the moment your soul chose to incarnate and it doesn't stop until your last breath. Don't rush it—it's a natural and gradual process.

Twelve Truths to a Spiritual Path
Truths One & Six will be repeatedly several times daily

*Truth One: Truth of Thoughts

Controlling of thoughts; Observing thoughts

Spiritual Practice

Keep a journal of what you said and what you thought. For one full day pay attention to your thoughts, the quality of your thoughts and the vibrations of your thoughts. Did you place blame on someone? Did you judge others?

This is useful information about yourself, don't judge it, but write it all down so you can really start observing your thoughts and what your inner dialogue is. This inner dialogue is how to speak to your inner child and why your life is the way it is. You created it. I have a spiritual TED (thoughts, emotions, desires) talk I engage in with every thought. It consists of the first three steps from my first book The Seven Gates: Seven Steps Beyond Self-Awareness. When I observe a negative thought entering my headspace, I have what I call a spiritual Ted talk with myself and ask three questions. The first question is if the thought is mother or father, the second question is what don't I like about the thought and the third question is what does it prove about me. When I can identify it is the unintegrated parent, that I am judging something I don't like in myself and that I'm simply trying to prove I'm unworthy, the thought goes away. This information allows me to see the low-level consciousness thoughts that I have and set them free.

Truth Two: Truth of Desire

Create space for spirit and matter equally

*Recognize your desires and how they're linked
to your values without judgement.*

Spiritual Practice

In every other culture there is a room for Spirit. It may be a closet or a shelf, but Spirit has importance in the person's life. In your personal space, create a place for Spirit.

Decorate it or not, it's up to you, it's to honor Spirit, which must be equal to the matter. Make room in your day for Spirit, just as you do for food, sleep, sex, and work. It may not be 50/50, but slowly increase the amount of time you dedicate to Spirit each day. This is reverence to Spirit and your inner child. Our desires will never subside, but when we give spirit more allowance in our lives there is a balance of earthly and spiritual desires. This is also a good time to add your inner child, either with a picture or a symbol, to the altar. The inner child got stuck in childhood and is waiting to get her needs met. When you make time for Spirit, you're in essence paying attention to your inner child.

When I have my spiritual TED talk, I ask what don't I like about the person, place, thing or situation. Whatever I'm judging is linked to my values. I have a saying "judgements are confessions, and they're great". Whatever I judge in this question is linked to what I value. Oftentimes our values are linked to things we deem negative like wealth or vanity. These are normal human desires and observation of our thoughts, judgements and values allows us to love ourselves despite these desires we judge. If you judge someone's appearance, perhaps you're vain and don't want to own it. Perhaps you judge privilege because you want wealth and you judge yourself as greedy. Honor these desires, they're normal. As long as we recognize that earthly desires are acceptable as 50% of life, we make room for the spiritual 50%.

TRUTH OF EMOTIONS & BREATH

Breathe, slow down, observe your judgements,
find a spiritual teacher, practice mirroring

SPIRITUAL PRACTICE

Again, control of the thoughts, but now not only observing them, but actually stopping to think about them and raising the vibration of the thoughts. Pay attention to the judgments you have.

Where do you do that same thing in your life: past, present, or future? This is called mirroring. Can you take a breath before saying something or when you catch yourself thinking negatively and ask where you have that same behavior (if you're judging someone)? Can you stop the negative self-talk and say it differently in a less negative way? This practice also has to do with the type of teacher you are seeking on your journey.

Emotions show up to teach us that we haven't processed certain thoughts about ourselves. Write a negative emotion on a piece of paper and crumble up the paper. Pass it over your body and see where you feel it. This will tell you where you hold that emotion. Hold it there and breathe through the emotion to feel it fully. Often when we fail to breathe it is because we don't want to feel the emotion for fear of it bringing up the past. Breathe through it fully and allow yourself to feel it, allowing the breath to guide you.

Seneca wrote "Without a ruler to do it against, you can't make crooked straight." Find someone to emulate, but pay attention that they're morally sound.

Pay very close attention that the teacher you're following isn't making false promises, isn't living the truth he/she preaches. Look at their life, does it resemble their teachings? Do they promise you fluff and easy techniques to your spiritual awakening?

Last, stop and take a break. Don't get sick, don't ask for permission. Schedule a break in your life. The world will continue on without you. If you don't schedule it, the universe will schedule it on demand through a physical or mental breakdown. Here you recognize that you are dual, and need to balance duality and unity.

A practice of *ho'oponopono*, while you take responsibility for yourself and the world you live in, can be a great practice in responsibility and forgiveness.

The lungs are represented by the child. We take our first breath as we leave our mother's body and we become a separate entity. When we don't breathe, talk fast or go into fight or flight, we aren't breathing and return back to child mode.

TRUTH FOUR: TRUTH OF INTUITION

Intuitive development

SPIRITUAL PRACTICE

This is about intuition. This does not mean you need to become intuitive, but paying attention to intuition is a subtle art. I like to say it is so subtle that it becomes a roar once you know how to listen.

I recommend the akashic records. You can take a class or teach yourself through books or online. Most of us are acting out of instinct and impulse. We react to a situation based on previous experiences and fear. It is our subconscious stuck at a point of trauma and we don't grow from there unless we take a breath, realize we are older now and not in danger. This is the intellect speaking.

It's the first step, then we transmute that intellect into wisdom. You get your instinct from the reptilian brain, your trauma, and your subconscious programming. When you start listening to your own inner voice, you start weeding out the noises and realize what the universe is really saying.

I recommend getting a symbol dictionary for learning myth, metaphor, and symbol. This is the language of the universe. Intuitive development or psychic development does not equal high consciousness. Your intuition will only be as clear as your level of consciousness. If you are living in chaos and in child mode that's the quality of guidance you'll get, do not kid yourself. Raise your vibration and your guidance will get much clearer.

Any intuitive art will teach you how to connect to your guidance and start listening more intently to the Universe. Try different ones out and see which one speaks to your soul.

Truth Five: Truth of Soul, Ego, Personality and Self-Love

Identifying the masks, you wear; why did you create that personality?
To compensate for what?

Here we start paying attention to the personality that we have created as a false way of getting our needs met.

We are all wearing masks, all the time. Your essence doesn't change, but your vibration can. What masks do you wear to people please? Be nice? Hide your true feelings. Debbie Ford has an excellent book called Why Good People do Bad Things which describes many of the masks we wear. I highly recommend it.

I recommend you finding the breakdown of your elements: air, earth, water, and fire and see which element is lacking or in excess

and see how you're overcompensating for that lack or excess in your astrological chart.

*Truth Six: Truth of Purification

Upgrade your diet and exercise routine.
Purify your body with a daily routine.

This is a time where shifting your diet and adding physical exercise may be of help.

If you've been truly changing your thoughts, a healthier diet, to balance your elements, is beneficial. For instance, I lack earth so I eat beets and sweet potatoes, which are root vegetables and bring in the earth element.

An ayurvedic practitioner would be a great resource here. Start dinacharya, a daily routine. This truth, along with the first truth, will be repeated until your last breath.

Anything that gets you moving or considering that your vessel holds the divine is a start to this truth. The more consideration we give to the body as the vehicle of the divine, the better we feel; however, in moderation. If you ignore your thoughts, a good diet will be useless. Seneca stated that if you make your body your master, you will have many slaves. There's more than the body and the form, but there is absolutely a place for care of the form because it is the dwelling of the Spirit. Illness is also an opportunity to get back into the body and in many traditions is viewed as an initiation to the spiritual path.

Truth Seven: Truth of Balance & Fun

Stop the pendulum swings of your thoughts and behaviors. Track the cycles of the pendulum swings. Return home to self.

This is all about starting to work toward equanimity and the 48 to 52. We all have four unmet needs: safety/security, protection, validation, and love. Love is everyone's main unmet need, however, discover which of the other three is the motor of your life.

Are you constantly seeking validation?

Are you in fight-flight to get your safety needs met?

Pick a word that describes your main theme in life, give that a 0, then find the exact opposite extreme and name it 100 and then find the 48 to 52 and name it. For instance, scarcity (0), abundant (100), efficiency (48 to 52). Inadequate (0), perfection (100), sufficient (48 to 52). This is going to be the main goal of your spiritual path: to try, with control of your thoughts, elements, personality, and intuition, to walk this path of 48 to 52 or as close to it as possible.

The Stoics had temperance as one of their main virtues. How can you find temperance in your swings of emotions and behaviors?

Truth Eight: Truth of the Shadow

Shadow Work

We all castrate one parent, the one we don't have the same power currency as and the one who holds the gold.

It's time here to do an inventory of what you don't like about that parent, mourn that you have those exact qualities, and start shadow work.

You have been imbalanced and creating strife to simply not accept that the qualities you disliked in that parent, which inevitably show up in your children, partners, and people you dislike who are mirroring you. This is an important time to take a break and mourn, **grieve what you have created in your life,** the suffering you've chosen not to rewrite the script, but rather, hide, pretending it isn't there.

This begins your return home to Self. This is the beginning of transmutation. We must raise our vibration. If we think we are going to solve the problem with the same level of vibration it was created at, we won't.

Here I invite you to ask your parents or family members about your moment of conception, your pregnancy, your birth story if you can and have access to it. If not, write down what happened to you between 0 to 7.

Most of us have one or two clear memories about that time in our life. Perhaps a sibling was born, a grandmother died, you moved countries or schools: write it down. Also, describe yourself as you remember yourself as a child, then write down how others described you as a child. The more information, the better.

The scenario between 0 and 7 will be the scenario you recreate in your life, based on themes, every seven years of your life. For instance, I got in trouble for creating a mess in the neighbor's pool and was kicked out of the family activities on Monday nights.

Every seven years I will create some mess that will get me kicked out of someplace. It can be a move, a divorce, a friendship or a job. It is not literal. It can be that I leave on my own accord, or I get dumped, but I created the situation to honor that story.

This is the depth of subconscious programming. Without this awareness there can be no true change. There's a great clip of the Hercules movie that shows the hydra and the gunk of the subconscious as the swamp. This step requires you to enter that subconscious swamp. NO TRUE SPIRITUAL GROWTH OCCURS WITHOUT THIS. I have free resources on my website, YouTube channel, and podcast to help you discover your subconscious patterns.

The best way that I have found to discover the shadow is to list the qualities of your parents you did not like between the ages of zero and seven, when the shadow was developing. You suppressed these shadow aspects to not accept you're like your parents and they're ruling your life. Start with acknowledging these aspects and begin a process of integrating these traits as part of who you are so you can be whole.

TRUTH NINE: TRUTH OF WISDOM & MENTORSHIP

*Identifying the external environment that's giving you
clues and guidance at all times.*

This step is the synchronicity step. Here you begin to see everything as guidance. Everything happening outside of you is inside of you.

This step is the synchronicity step. Here you begin to see every-thing as guidance. Everything happening outside of you is inside of you.

If there's a motorcycle speeding it may represent your thoughts racing or you going too fast. If the external environment is messy, you have chaos inside. Everything external is a mirror of your inner state. This step can seriously change your life and bring your intuition to a whole new level, not for guidance for others, but for yourself.

There is a rule I teach when teaching the Akashic Records "respond to all information given." This step reflects that same concept. Pay attention, the universe is talking to you at all times. The previous steps of listening to your thoughts, creating space for Spirit, knowing your subconscious patterns, and knowing you created everything in your life, culminate here. Pay attention and apply everything! The universe doesn't waste a moment, it all has meaning.

Milking the Moment is a good first step to develop this aspect of your guidance. Here you are merged with the universal consciousness and you realize that everything is connected. Synapses of the brain are firing and you're remembering many details from your childhood and making intuitive connections.

You soak up EVERYTHING as guidance; nothing escapes you or the universal law. However, you're still infantile here, thinking you change the world, that you can help someone and teach something to someone. You're still being the "teacher" or the guru by talking. Know that you are on your way to silence, which is a good thing.

Truth Ten: Truth of Simplicity and Silence

Silence, pilgrimage, and contemplation

This is the step of silence and pilgrimage.

This is the step of silence and pilgrimage.

In previous steps you were preaching, teaching, perhaps talking about your spiritual growth and having circles and ceremonies with friends. However, the changes up until now were to prepare you to vibrate at the level at which you are living, in silence.

You have preached, you've written the blogs or the books, you've offered the classes and people know what your beliefs are. Those who will follow you and want to learn from you will know you by your vibration, by living the teachings, not teaching the teachings. This step is about simplicity. Perhaps there are a few words of guidance you now share that sums up what you've learned. Provide small nuggets of wisdom and allow others to find their own path.

Teachings are taught with simplicity and in silence.

Many spiritual aspirants think they're here to save the world but cannot even save themselves. Prior to now, you have been learning about yourself, you have offered nothing to anyone, perhaps a word or advice, that you yourself needed, but you are not a healer.

Heal yourself first in the first nine steps, then in this step you begin to start helping humanity because you have truthfully transmuted into a higher vibrational being. Your external circumstances have changed and you are living your truth.

You are silent because there's no preaching necessary; everyone sees what you are. Here you can begin the last three steps: to help others. Only when you return home, know truthfully what you are and are not can you begin this step. I have made many pilgrimages, to Fatima and Lourdes, among others. You can do a small pilgrimage in your hometown to your favorite temple or church, or to a homeless shelter. It's representative of walking in silence.

You can also walk a labyrinth, my favorite contemplative practice. You can walk a finger labyrinth as well. Here you are clear about all of your thoughts and how they relate to others. You still have dogma, judgments, and criticisms; however, you immediately merge with the universal consciousness to see that you created it. You stop preaching here for you are living your truth and that speaks for itself. If you find yourself talking here, it is simply to state the certainty of your dogma, your theories, and owning them as a boundary.

Truth Eleven: Truth of Service

Serving humanity

This is the first step in helping humanity and being of service.

You cannot get here unless you have controlled and observed your thoughts, grown up your inner child, cultivated daily time to Spirit, balanced your energies, understood your subconscious fully and unified your consciousness with intellect and intuition, and have transmuted your vibration to a higher state of consciousness.

Once here you are of service to humanity in three ways: unselfish service, group work, and self-sacrifice for others. However, *not* at the expense of self.

Here you do not preach, your truth is your truth and do not impose it on others. This is the return to love. All dogma is transcended here. Everyone's "truth" is valid, yours no longer supersedes anyone else's. This leads you to Truth Twelve.

Truth Twelve: Truth of Unity

Unity with universal consciousness,
unity and no separation of Self with another

We come full circle from leaving home, balancing, returning home, understanding what our life has been and what role we played in it.

We forgave ourselves, forgave others, learned compassion and empathy, went into the world with Buddha or Christ consciousness, knowing who we truly are, and ready to serve with no expectations.

Here there are no judgments, criticisms, or beliefs that you are better than anyone or anyone is better than you. You don't need a parent because you understand you are the universe and the universe is you. This is a return to universal consciousness, the real womb and the real, un-cracked snow globe. No parents or hierarchy exist here. This is true union with God or the universe. This is you returning to the cosmic consciousness, while still remaining in the body. What started in Truth Two, the balance of Spirit and Matter, is now understood here. There is full symbiosis.

Myth: Hercules and the Capture of the Man-Eating Mares

Objective: Pay Attention to Your Thoughts

The man-eating mares are a metaphor for our thoughts. The Principle of Mentalism refers to our thoughts creating our reality. When we analyze our thoughts, we can create a new world. This is the first step in your spiritual journey.

Thought you observed. Conduct a spiritual TED talk when something that bothers you enters your head space by asking the following questions: 1. Was it your mother or father? 2. What didn't you like about it? 3. What does it prove about you?	
High Vibration (empathy, compassion, assertiveness)	
Low Vibration (criticism, judgement, lashing out)	

Was there a trigger? (i.e., weighing yourself and gaining a pound)	
Where did it happen? (i.e., at work, school, lingerie store)	
Can you link it back to another moment in your life? Preferably 0 to 7 years old.	
Can you find a theme in your thoughts?	

Myth: Hercules and the Capture of the Cretan Bull

Objective: Balance Spirit and Matter

The Cretan Bull symbolizes our dominion over matter. Spirit and the matter should be equal. In our material world we have forgotten to give equal time to Spirit.

<table>
<tr><td>Create a space for an altar or a space for quiet time for your spirit. What would you use to decorate it? What would it look like?</td><td></td></tr>
</table>

Name your inner child. Your inner child is a part of you that got stuck in negative childhood programming. You may have seen her get beat up in step one when you analyzed your thoughts.

Let's grow her/him up. Give her/him a name and a description. Draw a picture or find a picture of your younger self. Add her to your altar. What is her/his name?

What was your favorite fairy tale when you were younger? Can you identify the character in that fairy tale that is your spirit versus your matter?

For instance, my matter is Jafar; he is the egotistical maniac in the movie *Aladdin*. My spirit is the genie—funny and smart and gives good guidance.

What are your top two
values? Can you define
them in measurable terms?
How do you live up to
these values? How are your
judgements and desires
linked to these values?

Myth: Hercules and the Taking of the Golden Apples of the Garden of Hesperides

Objective: Notice your emotions, Breathe, Choose a Teacher Wisely & Schedule a Break

The Garden of Hesperides is guarded by a dragon, representing our lower thoughts. Hercules asks Atlas for help and Atlas gives Hercules the world to hold for a little while. Hercules takes a deep breath while he figures out how to defeat the dragon.

Pay attention to your breath. Take a deep breath, inhaling like Santa Claus and then hold your breath for four seconds, then exhale flattening your belly.	
Which did you prefer the inhale or the exhale? If you liked the exhale, you probably don't want to "take up space." If you preferred the inhale, perhaps you take up more space and push others out of the way.	
Both of these are child scripts of inferiority or superiority, both link to inadequacy. When you feel this coming on, stop and take a breath. It will take you out of fight-or-flight mode and into the rational mind.	

Who is your spiritual teacher? On YouTube, IG or at an ashram or a church, write their name here. Write down what qualities you admire about them. Ask yourself is this teacher truly walking the walk, or are they telling you to do something that they don't do themselves.

Does their life show they live the path they preach? Are they a Nereus or a Busiris? A Nereus nudges you in the right direction but doesn't make you reliant. A Busiris promises you the stars, and doesn't deliver, but keeps you dependent on them.

Schedule a break in your day to release yourself of your responsibilities. Schedule it here.

Who can you ask for help when your burdens get too great? Write their name here.

What low-level thoughts
are still plaguing you about
yourself? How can you raise
their vibration?

TRUTH FOUR: TRUTH OF INSTINCT, INTELLECT & INTUITION

Myth: Hercules and the Capture of the Ceryneian Doe

Objective: Switch from Instinct to Intelligence to Intuition

The Capture of the Ceryneian Doe is about transforming instinct (reptilian brain, fight-or- flight mode), into intelligence (rational thinking and breath control), into intuition (listening to our inner knowing).

How do you react under stress? Fight, flight, or freeze?	
Can you think of a moment in your childhood that causes this pattern to occur?	

<table>
<tr><td>

When a stressful situa-
tion arises can you stop
and breath, to get into the
intellect, before reacting?
If not, can you write what
the trigger was and what
your fear was that kept you
from breathing and thinking
clearly?

</td><td></td></tr>
<tr><td>

What does your rational
mind tell you about the
situation?

</td><td></td></tr>
</table>

Myth: Hercules and the Killing of the Nemean Lion

Objective: Your Soul's Purpose, Understanding Your Personality, the Ego and the Masks You Wear

The killing of the Nemean Lion requires self-analysis and honesty. Most of us have an accommodating personality that was created before we were seven to fit in and please others. Our soul is our true essence, the personality is necessary, but a mask we wear to fit it.

Describe your true essence in five words.	
Describe your personality in five words.	

What drives you? What do you do in an attempt to get validated? [Win awards, strive for perfection, make money, look good, wear expensive clothes, get straight A's] This is your ego and it is taking brilliance away from your soul. How can they work in tandem?	
Go online and find a free astrological chart. Calculate how many planets in air, fire, earth and water you have. Only use the moon, sun, Mercury, Mars, Venus, Jupiter, Saturn, Uranus, Neptune, and Pluto. You should have a total of ten, that's it. Add up the total elements to make sure you have ten. What is the breakdown?	Air: Fire: Earth: Water: Total:

Which is the element you have most of? How do you show up in a positive way with this element? How does your shadow show up? Air is linked to intellect, curiosity and openness; Water is linked to emotion and intuition; Earth is linked to security, and roots and Fire is linked to excitement and courage. Each element also has a shadow aspect. Air is linked to disassociation and detachment; Water is linked to depression and melancholy; Earth is linked to greed and an inability to take risks and Fire is linked to escapism and the "grass is greener" outlook.	
Which is the element you are lacking or have the least of?	
Describe how you over-compensate for the lacking element? For instance, if you lack earth to you overwork to make more money to feel grounded?	

How would your personality change if you lived to the truth of your elements in balance?

How can you return a bit closer to your true essence of your soul and kill a little of the personality and the mask you wear to not be "found out"?

Truth Six: Truth of Purification

Myth: Hercules and the Taking of the Girdle of Hippolyte, Queen of the Amazons

Objective: Begin a Healthcare Routine for the Body

The Girdle of Hippolyte is one of the labors in which Hercules messes up. We too will mess up on our path, it is inevitable. He went back and righted his wrongs. Every day we get an opportunity to do it all over again. This often refers to our lack of care for our physical body.

<table>
<tr><td>What one thing can you incorporate into your life to make yourself healthier?</td><td></td></tr>
</table>

How did your family take care of you when you were sick? Is there a correlation now to how you take care of yourself when you are sick? Is there a link to illness and allowing yourself off the hook for responsibilities?	
How do you purify your body when you have impure thoughts? Do you engage in abstinence from sex, food, shopping, drinking? Can you identify swings of unhealthy behaviors and how you purify by abstaining?	

TRUTH SEVEN: TRUTH OF BALANCE & FUN

Myth: Hercules and the Capture of the Erymanthian Boar

Objective: Find Your Equanimity, Your 48 to 52 and don't forget to laugh

The capture of the Erymanthian boar is the midpoint of your spiritual journey. Here you stop and reflect and make a plan of action for the remainder of the journey before you head back home. This is also the step for fun and laughter.

Which is your main unmet need from childhood: Safety/security, protection or validation?	

Can you remember the first time in childhood this need wasn't met? Can you identify how you recreate this in adulthood?

How do you show up for others in hopes of getting this need met?

Pick a word that describes your main theme in life, give that a 0, then find the exact opposite extreme and name it 100 and then find the 48 to 52 and name it. For instance, scarcity (0), abundance (100), efficiency (48 to 52). Inadequate (0), perfection (100), sufficient (48 to 52).	0	48 to 52	100
How can you add fun and laughter into your life? Can you laugh at certain things you've created because you were seeking attention or trying to get your needs met?			

Myth: Hercules and Destroying the Lernaean Hydra

Objective: Enter the Shadow which begins your return home to Self

This is the beginning of transmutation. We must raise our vibration from the moment of conception. Destroying the Lernaean Hydra represents the first step toward the return home. You must confront your shadow, admit you have been pretending to be something you're not, and begin integrating the un-integrated parent.

What qualities didn't you like about your mother as a child?	
What qualities didn't you like about your father as a child?	

What are the qualities in others you find yourself judging?

Which parent do you share a power currency with? Which parent was overt power? Which was covert power? Which is your preferred power currency? How can you integrate the opposite power currency

Can you see that you have these same qualities in your life?

Myth: Hercules and the Killing of the Stymphalian Birds

Objective: This Step is the Synchronicity Step Where You Begin to See Everything as Guidance; Everything Happening Outside of You is Inside of You

The killing of the Stymphalian Birds refers to using the higher mind, the universal mind, to guide us. This refers to the Law or Correspondence.

<table>
<tr><td>Use the adage "as within, so without" daily. What did you discover was outside that you could link to what was going on for you internally?</td><td></td></tr>
</table>

Use "Milking the Moment" to be guided by your inner wisdom and higher mind. Set an alarm clock every day at the same time. When it goes off pay attention to what you're listening to, what you're saying, or what you're thinking. This is your higher mind giving you guidance. What did you learn from your inner wisdom today?

Myth: Hercules and the Slaying of Cerberus Guardian of Hades

Objective: This Step is About Silence, Pilgrimage, and Contemplation

The slaying of Cerberus, Guardian of Hades, refers to being in silence and teaching through your high vibration. Many aspirants like to embark on a pilgrimage, a silent retreat, or walk a labyrinth as a contemplative practice.

Sit in silence. What did you discover about yourself?	
Walk a labyrinth, either a walking or a finger labyrinth. What did you learn about yourself? To find a labyrinth near you go to www. labyrinthlocator.com or print a paper labyrinth.	

Go on a silence retreat or
take a break from the world,
as in a vision quest or take
a walk in nature. What did
you discover?

What are your teaching
through your "vibration"
now, which you no longer
need to speak about?

Has anyone noticed a
change in you? What have
they said?

Myth: Hercules and the Cleaning of the Augean Stables

Objective: Serving Humanity by Using Your Resources Wisely (Time, Money, Energy) and Not Depleting Yourself to Serve Others; In This Both You and Others Are Served

The cleaning of the Augean Stables refers to helping to clean up the world you created by your past deeds and thoughts. We don't go backward here and give in excess to meet our unmet needs from childhood. We are helping others with no desire for anything in return.

How can you give back with unselfish service? Where you and the other both gain?	

How can you participate in group work?

Perhaps an organization with a mission you believe in, not as a leader, but as a follower.

How can you sacrifice some of your time and money, that you have a surplus of, but not taking from yourself and your needs. For instance, if you have some extra money after all of your bills are paid, then you can donate to a cause. Do not take what you need for your needs to give to others.

Myth: Hercules and the Capture of the Red Cattle of Geryon

Objective: This Is Union and Wholeness in Self and Toward Others

This is where Spirit rules matter. We have come full circle. Initially we left home, balanced ourselves, and returned home. In so doing, we gained clarity about what our life has been and what role we played in it. We forgave ourselves, forgave others, learned compassion and empathy, and went into the world with Buddha or Christ consciousness, knowing who we truly are. Now we're ready to serve, with no expectations. Draw a picture of what is in your heart as you reach this truth. What do you wish to leave the world from this heart space?